peoplework

people work

Austin
Allison
·
Chris
Smith

This book would not exist without the following people:

Peoplework was edited by Georgina
Chong-You and Lauren Schuster

Peoplework was designed by Mike Mangigian

Peoplework was produced by dotloop

Peoplework was published by Peoplework, LLC

Special thanks to LaunchSquad, 1000Watt, Alex Allison,
Nathan Scherotter and our Kickstarter backers.

The Peoplework principles were developed inside the
walls of dotloop by the people who work there. The actions
they take each day are what inspired this movement.

First Edition
Publication date January 15th, 2014

ISBN: 978-0-9911730-0-6

Acknowledgment

In order to do great things, you need great people alongside you.

To our families, friends and colleagues who support us each and every day...You are the people we work so hard for.

The Principles of Peoplework

FOREWORD   8

INTRODUCTION   10

Principle 1

P2P REPLACES B2B AND B2C   12

Principle 2

HUMAN COMPANIES WIN   30

Principle 3

CHANGE REQUIRES A BLUEPRINT   46

Principle 4

PURPOSE BEFORE TECHNOLOGY   62

Principle 5

QUALITY CREATES QUANTITY   78

Principle 6

SERVICE IS MARKETING   94

Principle 7

BUSINESSES ARE BUILT ON COMMUNITIES   106

Principle 8

PASSION POWERS PROFITS   122

Principle 9

STARS ARE MADE IN HOLLYWOOD   134

Principle 10

ONLY YOU WRITE YOUR STORY   148

You aren't addicted to social media, or your phone, you are addicted to people.

In 2006, I started a daily video blog called "Wine Library TV," where I recorded five episodes a week for five and a half years. I think the only person who watched the first episode was my mom. I used platforms like Wordpress, YouTube, Tumblr, Twitter and Facebook before most people even knew they existed. Truth be told, I had no idea what I was doing or if it would "work."

But I hustled, I was passionate and I was keenly aware of my DNA (for better or worse). These are the primary three reasons why the audience grew.

Genuine relationships formed and, eventually, tens of thousands of people started to tune in. I built my brand (and business) around a passionate community of like-minded people. My only real goal in using the "platforms" was to find people to listen to (and who might want to listen to me, too).

In the last four years I've written three New York Times best sellers (Crush It!, The Thank You Economy and Jab, Jab, Jab, Right Hook). I regularly speak at conferences that pay me fifty-thousand dollars for an hour keynote. I also started a social media agency, VaynerMedia, where we are humbled to call GE and the New York Jets clients and where we have grown to more than 300 employees.

None of this would have even been possible ten years ago. The newly established "people grid" you will read about in Peoplework is very real. It provides (and has already provided me) unprecedented opportunities.

Because of my documented digital success, people and companies now turn to me every day asking, "How can I use social media more effectively right now to grow my business like you did?" and "Which social networks do we have to be on next year?"

Here's what they are actually asking: "How can I better understand and communicate with people right now?" and "Where will people be connecting and interacting with other people next year?"

Austin and Chris put people first. So will the most successful businesses during the next decade (and beyond). They (and you) should focus on people, not just platforms and pixels.

Gary Vaynerchuk
@garyvee

WHAT IS PEOPLEWORK?

Peoplework is a better way to run a business by putting people first in a digital-first world. Peoplework is the new revolution — a post-industrial and post-digital revolution that we are calling the "people revolution." Access to the distribution of products and services has become ubiquitous. The people revolution, combined with the impact of the digital revolution, provides more people than ever before with access to other people. This new "people grid," much like the electrical grid before it, brings a tremendous opportunity.

Peoplework consists of ten timeless business principles that clearly define how any business now can work better together with more people than ever before. Much of this is thanks to recent innovation and the highly digital, constantly connected world around us. Apple products, Google searches, Facebook friends, Twitter hashtags and the many other ways we connect have glued us all together, and created a new online society. During the people revolution, there will be more collaboration between an ever-growing community using these established digital connections. As time passes, however, the experience will be much less mechanical and linear, while becoming more real and natural.

The ten Peoplework principles defined in this book are the blueprint for this unprecedented opportunity in time. Companies who run their organizations using the Peoplework principles now have a competitive advantage comparable to the companies who were at the forefront of the industrial and digital revolutions. Digital tools and technology are the catalysts and enablers of prosperity for Peoplework businesses. The goal is to focus on people — your customers and your employees. The ability to retain a customer, and their lifetime value to your business, has never been more important than it is during the people revolution. The people who comprise your workforce will matter more to your successes, or failures, than ever before. Welcome to Peoplework!

Principle 1

PEOPLE TO PEOPLE REPLACES
BUSINESS TO BUSINESS AND
BUSINESS TO CONSUMER

ALONE WE CAN DO SO LITTLE;
TOGETHER WE CAN DO SO MUCH.

-HELEN KELLER

In the pre-digital revolution, there were limited fractures in the communication chain. Before the twentieth century, if you wanted to buy just about anything (land, professional services, retail products) you would meet the person or business selling the product face-to-face. It was a simple way of working together. The terms of sale and all other pertinent details were established while we were "belly to belly." Then, you would come to an agreement, or not, and part ways. Deals truly got done in "real time," and the more people-to-people (P2P) interactions you had, the more sales you made. The bottom line? Sales always have and always will happen when two or more people work together without friction. Period.

The digital revolution established a grid, a digital foundation, and this grid can build and grow any business to unprecedented scale. Without the digital grid, the only option was meeting face-to-face, which resulted in arguably fewer frustrations than there are today. It is how we react to these new, and often initially frustrating, ways of communicating that will define us during the people revolution. Will we accept digital interjections, while still embracing the face-to-face interactions of the good ole days, in order to see results? The answer is yes…Peoplework!

Our grandfathers would call Peoplework common sense. Physically connecting with another individual creates the ability to sell without using a machine as the mediator. Today, however, here is what would typically unfold: We would begin by talking on the phone, likely after several missed calls/voicemails, and then we would exchange text messages. As things progressed, we would bounce back and forth several lengthy e-mails, and along the way, we even manage to connect on a few popular social networks.

The irony of course, through all of this digital correspondence, is we would likely conclude that we never even need to meet in person.

Our grandfathers, used to the old business model, would likely find this scenario frustrating. So, is there a way to juxtapose the post-digital revolution with the ways of old?

Absolutely! This is the goal of Peoplework, which is only now possible thanks to the rapid advancement of technology during the last decade. Peoplework is about getting back to basics, with a digital twist.

The concept of Peoplework is as important as the Internet is to a business. It provides a change in the way people interact with one another and the way businesses operate. The people revolution is a new era that provides opportunities to put people first in a technology-driven world. The sooner you become a Peoplework business, the more you will gain.

A Digital Landscape

Smart phones and tablets have created anytime, real-time connections. They also provide access to unlimited information. Thanks to massive digital innovation during the twenty-first century, we can work from any Starbucks with any other person on the planet. Inconveniently, however, we have more usernames and passwords than we do customers! As a result, the same things that connected us, in many ways, disconnected us by creating physical barriers. Sure, we are always connected, we never turn off; we also never look up to see who is standing right in front of us.

WE ARE ALWAYS CONNECTED, WE NEVER TURN OFF; WE ALSO NEVER LOOK UP TO SEE WHO IS STANDING RIGHT IN FRONT OF US

Accidents occur on a daily basis as a result of being so fully consumed by our digital connections. Watch any congested pedestrian area and you will see people so engrossed in their electronics that they run into things, or do a quick search on YouTube for "woman falling in fountain at mall." We are a people always on the go, but we never leave anything behind. In the Peoplework era, we utilize digital means to work together...again.

In hindsight, while the industrial revolution brought us to today's modernized society, it also set us up for a tremendously inefficient transition to a digital and mobile world (i.e., the printing press versus a thumb drive, telephone poles versus satellites). Most companies and entrepreneurs are focusing on the digital revolution and the influx of technological innovation as the revolution that matters. After all, a mobile-first society is officially the new normal, if you haven't noticed. So companies are racing as quickly as they can to digitize their existing processes. Digitization, however, is just a moment in time on a larger Darwinistic journey.

DIGITIZATION IS JUST A MOMENT IN TIME ON A LARGER DARWINISTIC JOURNEY

Technology is not the destination, but it is a powerful tool, like fire once was, that propels people forward. The sooner organizations realize that technology simply enables you to work better with people, and then refocus on said people, the sooner they will thrive. You can't ignore technology in business in the same way that you can't ignore people in business. Our goal is to get you to merge the two while elevating the value of people-to-people interaction.

The beauty of the industrial revolution was that the rate of growth, the rate of production and the speed of delivery became faster than ever. Essentially, the power grid went mainstream. For the first time, it truly felt like what we now call a "first-world society." Machines, not people, were producing the goods for the big companies. Being at the forefront of the industrial revolution allowed people like the Rockefellers, and their businesses, to become legendary.

The first people to access the power grid won and won big. Once the grid was generally accessible, however, the modern world expected power. It was no longer a sales benefit or unique value proposition that a company kept the lights on. Things that were once a company's biggest competitive advantage, like access to technology or social media channels today, instantly were not.

This is exactly what will happen in the people revolution. Your mobile app and strong API might help you win now, but those days are numbered. It's back to basics and basics involve humans.

IT'S BACK TO BASICS AND BASICS INVOLVE HUMANS

Now, understand that we're not rejecting the digital revolution altogether. Smart phones, instant messages, social media and online interactions have all made connections with people easier, globally possible and downright more fun. However, it has also brought a level of diminished capacity to our genuine people-to-people connections. Do not let all the shiny objects fool you, people still just want to work as efficiently as possible with other people.

Sure, everything is now digital, and everyone is now connected, but no matter what you sell or do for a living, one thing we still know is that it involves people on both sides. The key to success in the people revolution is to understand that technology has simply changed the way that people work together. How do we work better with people in a technology-enabled, digital world? We do this by shifting the focus off of pixels and putting it back on people.

The Birth Of The Microwave Mentality

As the digital revolution began, time as a factor was slowly eliminated. The ability to pick up a phone and instantly talk to someone on the other side of the country was a game changer. Imagine how fascinating it was to use a fax machine for the first time. Today, we joke about people still faxing, but the ability to eliminate lag time between physical communication was what made the digital revolution so special. However, it gave the world a microwave mentality — push a button and instantly send or receive messages. Since everything is digital and everything is online, so many consumers now have zero patience. The digital revolution has been the focus of most companies within our era, but the Peoplework revolution is all about people working better together, post-digital. The impact of Peoplework will be as dramatic for the companies that get people right as it was for the companies who got machines and mega pixels right.

So, why is it beneficial for you to go paperless? Does less paper really fulfill your end goal? The answer is usually no. At our company, dotloop, we help real estate professionals go "paperless." At least that's how people talk about it. What we really do is replace paperwork with Peoplework, which never would have been possible before the people revolution. The demand is here, and Peoplework will replace paperwork, period. Technology is simply the enabler to a better experience between two or more people.

In the case of dotloop, we help real estate professionals and companies work better together by putting people first in a digital- first world. It's not about technology; it's about people. The problem is that most people start by asking the wrong questions.

Most of our customers want to know more about running a better business (faster, more secure, mobile) and less about paperwork. But traditional logic tells us that "paperless" is what we need. This backward, digitization-focused approach to the selection of business tools has hurt many companies' bottom lines. The truth is, like most businesses, real estate agents do not want to "go paperless," they want to work better with their clients. The logic is very simple: If you're doing better work with your clients, they will keep coming back for more and tell their friends about it. Given that the most profitable source of new business is referrals, Peoplework, not paperwork, generates big returns over time. Having a clear understanding of people-focused technology is essential in a people-first world.

A New Mindset

As much as the digital revolution increased connectedness, it equally created a new kind of distance. Frustration, inefficiency and miscommunication led to deals falling apart and numerous businesses failing across every industry. The world was changing and, though the digital grid enabled people to work with more people, it did not tell them how. Belly to belly is still possible, but requires a new mindset and a new definition in the Peoplework era. The inability for most businesses to adapt to this people revolution is not the fault of the business or any fault of our own. There is no college degree or MBA that teaches you how to be a Peoplework company. Traditionally, if you wanted to be a businessperson, your education focused (and still focuses) on the business part only — numbers and profit margins — not the person part — communicating with people. Schools of business universally teach things like finance, marketing, sales and operations. Truthfully, there isn't anything you learned in school that will make you successful during the people revolution. The majority of the ways people are able to work better together now did not even exist five years ago. Business is no longer about financial accounting or learning how to be good at streamlining operations, it's about people optimization!

Becoming A People-to-People Company

In the people revolution, amazing customer service, genuinely caring about your customers, humanizing your brand publicly and poignant storytelling are what will produce profits and customers who will send you more customers. These customer experiences will frequently happen inside of websites, text messages, emails, videos, mobile applications and social media platforms. Being a Peoplework business is not about mastering the touch-screen or growing a huge social network following, it is about people working better with people. Being human, being accessible and being genuine within these new digital channels is where you win, or lose, as a business for the next decade and beyond. The technology and digital elements of this people revolution are no different from the time of having early access to electricity. So, since technology is now ubiquitous, how do you win as a business? First, you must understand that since the beginning of time, and forever into the future, people just want to work with other people and will more often than not choose people who they know, like and trust. No matter what the business model or product is, it is always people on both sides of the transaction.

NO MATTER WHAT THE BUSINESS MODEL OR PRODUCT IS, IT IS ALWAYS PEOPLE ON BOTH SIDES OF THE TRANSACTION

The digital revolution as we knew it is ending and the people revolution is beginning what will be a multi-decade journey. Simply digitizing existing processes is not the endgame moving forward. Rather, it is effectively communicating and working with people in a digital-first world. As an example, taking your database from a shoebox with index cards and putting it online isn't enough in the people revolution.

The digital revolution is very similar to the electrical grid. It used to be an obvious competitive advantage for a hotel chain to advertise having lights, but soon every hotel had lights. Businesses had to offer something that grabbed attention, something that had staying power. Fast-forward to today and we get warm cookies, free nights and rock-bottom prices using mobile applications like Hotwire and Hotel Tonight.

The trend today is that companies are screaming as loud as they can about their social media presence or mobile application. We hear a constant stream of social media commands: *Follow us on Twitter. Like us on Facebook. Subscribe to our YouTube channel. Download our iPhone and Android applications. Subscribe to our Blog. Follow us on Instagram.* In the people revolution, all of that is akin to a hotel long ago saying, "We have lights." It's what comes next that truly matters.

The digital revolution was a positive thing and has undeniably improved the ways that we communicate. However, it wasn't the pot of gold at the end of the rainbow that many expected it to be. As it turns out, there was, and is, more. There's the people side.

When you look at your business strategies through this lens, it forces you always to start with people. People to people (P2P) is a better way of looking at our digital and highly connected world, while combining the collaborative process of people working and communicating together.

Everyone Needs Peoplework

Technology has become ubiquitous — everyone with a smart phone is two clicks away from everyone else on the planet. As a result, every industry must change.

The reason the digital revolution is so critical to the people revolution is that it brought big ideas to scale... instantly. Digital is what created the people-to-people ecosystem. Think about Instagram, a mobile-first social network for photos, which was adopted by millions almost instantly following its inception. This is an example of a product of the people revolution. Kodak couldn't even have manufactured enough cameras to keep up with the demand Instagram faced. In comparison, what makes Twitter so "cool" is that, in 140 characters or less, people get to rapidly share their thoughts, ideas and passions with others. Without all of these people, Twitter would be empty. Likewise, Facebook is also useless without people, and YouTube would be nothing if not for the people who contribute content to the platform. You get the point. We have gone from a web of pages to a web of people.

WE HAVE GONE FROM A WEB OF
PAGES TO A WEB OF PEOPLE

These P2P trends are just the beginning of what we will see in the people era.

Resistance Is Futile

When Facebook started to grow, it was largely about what people were eating for breakfast, and less about connecting with people on a real level. Because of this, many logged on for the first time and then instantly logged off, deeming it stupid. But once Grandma (and everyone else) realized that if she wanted to watch her grandchildren grow up or wanted to connect with a friend or family member in another state or country, she needed to be on Facebook.

Uploading pictures to your timeline and tagging your friends and family in photos will always be important regardless of what website or mobile app we do it in, but it goes much further. When we were just a startup, it was the people who rallied behind dotloop that helped us to be selected by Keller Williams, the largest real-estate company in North America. [i] They chose people, not pixels. At that time, there were much older and more established alternatives, but Keller Williams believed that Peoplework, and not paperwork, would be the differentiator in the people era. It is critical that we build businesses for the sake of people, not for the sake of pixels.

Businesses in the people era should be enablers of people communicating more effectively and efficiently with other people, inside these new and exciting digital channels.

Flip The Funnel

Throughout all three revolutions, industrial, digital and people, people work with people. The platform may change, the expectations may change, but it is always going to be people working together. It is critical to understand business-to-business (B2B) and business-to-consumer (B2C), because through them we will truly understand people to people.

B2B historically has understood "people" better than B2C. People like Jack Welch and Zig Ziglar have long been teaching about the benefits to a business in having strong business relationships. B2C used to be about location, location, location. The more eyes on it, the more money the business made. For example, the most important thing for a Best Buy brick-and-mortar store was its location. The most important thing for a cereal was its shelf placement at the grocery store.

Today, thanks to the people revolution, the entire value proposition has changed. Now, people go to Apple because they are passionate about the brand, not because it is at the mall. In fact, they go to the mall now because there is an Apple Store. Whole Foods is often not conveniently located, but people journey there because they have a commitment to quality and a culture that resonates deeply with their loyal customers. In the past, Macy's was the reason people came to the mall; now Macy's needs Apple and Target needs Whole Foods. The brands focused on people and culture have become the anchor stores!

PEOPLE GO T O APPLE BECAUSE THEY ARE PASSIONATE ABOUT THE BRAND, NOT BECAUSE IT IS AT THE MALL

If you're not convinced, let's take a look at a surprising example: breakfast cereal. Surely breakfast cereal isn't in the P2P business, right? Wrong. Even something as simple as a box of cereal defies the rules when people are passionate enough about the product. Kashi is a great example of a brand that typically would have had nowhere to go, but, because people connected with people (specifically, organic food lovers), Kashi now determines its placement on shelves, not the other way around. Prior to Kashi, Frosted Flakes and Cheerios were all you used to see. P2P even changed the cereal game. Now a company's ability to connect with the people it serves is the differentiator and accelerator.

The Rebirth of People

P2P has also changed the relationships that people have with their companies. People used to work at the same company for the duration of their career. The relationship ended when one of the two parties died or retired. Today, we've gone from thirty-year jobs that people wore like a badge of honor to three-year jobs that seem like someone stayed for a "long" time. The only real value in staying with your company forever was that you knew you had a job that was secure. In the people revolution, you do not even need to be a "company" to be a business.

The world's largest industries are being disrupted by the people revolution. Traditional business models of today will eventually no longer exist, including the gold standards within sectors like labor, transportation, retail, travel, housing, banking and education. No one is immune to people.

NO ONE IS IMMUNE TO PEOPLE

The new business models in the people era will put people first and not rely on the securities implied by traditional B2B and B2C models.
Let us look at what is happening within a few newer people-to-people business models. In the past, if I wanted to hire someone to do web design, I hired a web design firm. Today, I use a company like Elance to choose from a pool of skilled freelance web designers, and find the one who matches my needs. We used Elance to hire Georgina Chong-You, a highly skilled content and copy editor, for the book you are reading right now, because she was the right person for the job. In the past, if I wanted someone to clean my home, I hired Merry Maids or a professional cleaning service. Today, I use TaskRabbit to hire
a person. If I needed a ride to the airport, I called a car service. Today, I use Lyft or Uber or Get Around. I used to go to a jewelry store to buy jewelry. Now I use Etsy and buy jewelry from an individual. Every industry is at war.

There was always competition for business, but now it comes from other people and from more businesses. Many of these people and companies want to focus more on people instead of profit. This is the people revolution.

If you look at each of these verticals, and the transactions within them, there's a common theme: people just want to work with other qualified people to accomplish a goal.

The Great Myth

The great myth is that we preferred to work with a company in the first place. We believed that it would be somehow more risky to work with an individual, and not a business or an established brand. After all, a "real" business has more infrastructure, more staff, more marketing dollars and more physical space, therefore, they must be better, right? Wrong. Today, all of those things are considered tremendous liabilities, not assets. Honestly, why work with a design firm when I could simply work with a person who I knew was right for the job? Before the digital and people revolutions, websites like those profiled in our Case Studies section below could not have existed. People were never connected to the degree necessary to disrupt the monumental business ecosystems built over the last few centuries. Now, technology has made this disruption not only possible, but also global and immediate.

Technology is not a bad thing; it doesn't put a damper on success. The key is to utilize it to your advantage, while remembering that success is fueled by people serving people. Institutions are out, and individuals are in.

INSTITUTIONS ARE OUT, INDIVIDUALS ARE IN

CASE STUDIES

PEOPLE-TO-PEOPLE IN ACTION

Airbnb

People who want to rent a property while on vacation can connect with other people looking to rent their space through an online marketplace called Airbnb (Air Bed & Breakfast). This marketplace is made up of "Hosts" and "Guests" who register with Airbnb and create a user profile on the website. There is also a private messaging system that every Host or Guest can use to connect with each other within the site.

In addition to the personal information Hosts provide on their profile, they also list details about their property, such as: price per night, house rules, neighborhood information, amenities, and images.

The concept of Airbnb was created by Brian Chesky and Joe Gebbia in 2008. In an effort to pay their own rent, roommates Chesky and Gebbia turned their living room into a bed and breakfast, providing air mattresses and a homemade breakfast for their three guests. One year later, the online marketplace expanded beyond air mattresses to homes, castles, boats, manors, tipis, igloos and private islands. The company has continued to grow and by February 2011 they reached one million booked listings with a 65% increase in revenue. Airbnb has also received celebrity recognition: first, by actor Ashton Kutcher announcing a significant investment in the company; and second, by partnering with NYC Mayor Michael Bloomberg to offer free housing to persons displaced by Hurricane Sandy in 2012. [ii]

TaskRabbit

TaskRabbit, founded by former IBM software engineer Leah Busque in 2008, is an online and mobile marketplace allowing its users to outsource odd jobs to people in their neighborhood or surrounding area. It is an on-demand delivery network that hires people to complete tasks for other people. Since its inception, TaskRabbit has received $37.5 million in funding and has been described as the "eBay for real-world labor."

According to Busque, the idea for a task-running website came on a cold, snowy evening in February 2008, when she and her husband realized they were out of dog food. Later that night, after discussing how much she'd be willing to pay someone to pick up dog food for her, RunMyErrand.com was born. The service, now called TaskRabbit, runs by having clients type in a task, name a price and see a list of TaskRabbits to choose from to complete the job.

Busque sees her company as a technology platform that changes the very concept of neighborliness. She said, "People have said that TaskRabbit is bringing it back, allowing people to connect [with] their neighbors again."

TaskRabbit was nominated for TechCrunch's Best Mobile App of 2011, and Busque was nominated for Founder of the Year. TaskRabbit has also been profiled in publications like The New York Times and The Guardian. [iii]

Kickstarter

In 2009, a private web-based American company called Kickstarter launched, providing a means to raise money for creative projects via crowd funding.

Kickstarter has funded feature films, music, stage shows, comics, journalism, video games, and food-related projects. Crowd funding means that individuals can monetarily back projects in exchange for a tangible reward or one-of-a-kind experience. These experiences can be a personal note of thanks, dinner with an author, or first printed copy of a book. Creators must give a complete description of their project and educate their audience about the project goals in order to encourage contributions.

Kickstarter is not a traditional avenue of investment. Money is pledged by donors from anywhere in the world and collected using Amazon payments. In order for Kickstarter project creators to collect their money, they must set a funding goal and meet that goal by the set deadline. Only the creators own the projects, and Kickstarter takes 5% of the funds raised. This very book, Peoplework, began as a Kickstarter project. We exceeded our funding goal of $50,000 by raising $73,280 in just 30 days.

Kickstarter is completely serviced and backed by people. People are not placing orders for a product, rather, they are helping to underscore projects. Kickstarter allows creators and their audience to work together. [iv]

These people-to-people focused business models and technologies have not only enabled us to connect directly to people when we buy or hire, they are arguably a safer bet. Remember, the grid is now the status quo!

HUMAN COMPANIES WIN

 I'M NOT A BUSINESSMAN.
I'M A BUSINESS, MAN.

-JAY Z

Historically, people have thought about businesses like business, where revenue, expenses and cost sheets dominate their thoughts, time and meeting agendas. This does not, however, leave much room for people. To be a Peoplework company you need to think about your business through the lens of a human being, not an Excel doc.

Building genuine friendships and building a successful business are not all that different. Stop for a minute and think about the reasons that you enjoy spending time with your family and friends. I'm sure that as you think about those reasons, a smile comes across your face. Yet, your thoughts about business don't evoke the same thoughts or responses. For some reason, it's not typical to think about businesses like people. Peoplework businesses understand that they need to be human. Business traits during the people revolution should be human, like honesty, transparency, forgiveness, and encompassing of a genuine personality. If you were moving to a new city, how would you make friends? You would be human; you would be yourself, and never look at them as a transaction. The goal of friendship is a lifetime bond, not a quick buck.

THE GOAL OF FRIENDSHIP IS A LIFETIME BOND, NOT A QUICK BUCK

A Peoplework company thinks about its customers very much the same way, like friends and family. Why? Because people connect with humanity. So being a human business means that you'll more effectively connect with your customers.

Blood Is Thicker Than Water

Family is the best model for lifetime retention, period. The family model works because we care about our family and you treat the people you care about differently. When you run a human business, you care about your customers like family. This is what will make you a Peoplework business, and since the entire digital "grid" is made up of people, only human companies can win.

Friends are similar, building on the same foundation that makes familial bonds so strong. A deep level of care, trust and transparency is required for a strong friendship. And over time, not only does the level of trust grow between friends, but more things surface as well. For example, close friends start to develop common passions and interests over time. Imagine if your customers became as passionate as you about your business. Unlike family, an added benefit to friendship is that you get to choose who your friends are! Peoplework businesses choose their customers.

PEOPLEWORK BUSINESSES CHOOSE THEIR CUSTOMERS

You're probably thinking, "But I do care about my customers." Ask that in the context of how you care about your friends. If a friend called and was in a bind unable to pick up their daughter from school, you would not start calculating reimbursement for the miles you would have to drive. You would do everything in your power to help them because you care. Caring shows that we are human, and we all want to be cared about. Let me be clear though, not all friends get the same amount of care, because that doesn't scale. All friends do not get the same treatment, nor can all customers, but they all can be treated with genuine respect and selflessness. Whether it's friends, family or customers, treat them like you care and lifetime relationships will follow.

The Human Factor

What makes people want to work with other people? Flaws,

freckles and humor make a human unique and they are also what helps a business win. Genuine morals and values, plus knowing exactly whom you want to attract to your business, will go a long way in the people revolution. Having a loyal customer base is the driving force of a people-first business. Moreover, a loyal customer base happens when you understand people.

A LOYAL CUSTOMER BASE HAPPENS WHEN YOU UNDERSTAND PEOPLE

Being a human company allows you to attract customers who will be with you through thick and thin because they know you have their back as well. Customers will be loyal to your business like they are loyal to their family.

Bottom line: it is not personal or business anymore, it is YOU. In eras past, we would play golf, even if we hated it, because that is what you did to fit into the business crowd. Personally, I love playing sports and watching them from time to time, but it would be a stretch to call me a sports fan. Traditional logic would suggest this was a problem given that nearly every man on the planet follows sports avidly. I couldn't count the number of times I've walked into a meeting or networking event where someone struck up a conversation with me not knowing that I didnt have a clue what he or she was talking about. When it happens, I don't try to be something that I'm not, I simply say, "Sorry, I don't follow sports," and try to pick up a new topic of discussion. I am who I am and I'll spend my time on things that interest me; sports don't make that list. When you are a human company, you do not have to pretend to be something that you are not.

Academic books are not written about how to be a human company, but you must begin somewhere. The same precepts that apply to connecting with people and the basic responsibilities of being a human should apply to business too. It is much easier said than done, however, because we've been trained a certain way for years. You go to business school, where you learn about marketing, finance and law. Compare that to a human being. We are taught general wellness, personal hygiene and the importance of obeying the law of the land. Traditional education does not tell us how to be a likable person with lots of friends. We learn that on our own, by being human, making mistakes, showing that we care, and developing emotional, and sometimes physical, connections with the people around us.

Most businesses think only about quantity, while most humans think about the quality first. Once you start thinking about your business and your work like your personality and your friendships, you have crossed the first hurdle. When your business is human, it creates infinite opportunities.

WHEN YOUR BUSINESS IS HUMAN, IT CREATES INFINITE OPPORTUNITIES

An Early Life Lesson

When you apply the human touch to your business, you must keep in mind that humans are not perfect. In my teenage years, I was headed down a bad path. I made a number of poor choices and, at the time, was unable to see their negative impact on other people's lives. These choices led me to fail several classes, nearly flunk out of high school, and become involved with illegal substances. My only close friends were the ones who supported my bad habits, and I lost sight of the people who really cared about me. The apex, near the end of my sophomore year of high school, ended in a serious conviction and jail time at sixteen years of age. Thankfully, I had family and friends who cared for me, and that moment taught me that my choices and actions would determine where I was going to go in life. As I looked in the mirror, I realized that I wanted to have a positive, not a negative, impact on the lives of people around me. So, from that moment on, I committed my life to doing just that.

Following this life event, I graduated number one in my class at the University of Cincinnati and earned an academic scholarship into a top-tier law school at the Cincinnati College of Law. After that, I started dotloop, which has become the fastest growing software company in the history of the real estate industry. I've also been named Innovator of the Year in my industry, included in the Forbes 30 under 30 list and featured on the cover of Entrepreneur Magazine. These accomplishments are humbling and didn't come without a lot of sacrifice and hard work, but I owe it all to the people around me and the life lesson that I learned during my troubled teenage years.

This story about my youth is part of who I am. So why hide it? Although I may not lead with this childhood memory in sales pitches or with the media, I'm not ashamed of it either. I made mistakes, I owned up to them, I learned from them and I became a better person as a result. Human businesses think about their imperfections in the very same way and become better in time by being themselves.

Humility and transparency are a part of what makes us all human. Likewise, in becoming a human company you must be humble and transparent. No one is perfect, so why pretend to be? The same is true of every business. Share your vision and values far and wide. In business, when you make a mistake, don't hide it. Rather, show humility and own up to it. Oftentimes this will need to happen publicly. When a mistake impacts your customers, make it right. In a human company, it is not about who is right. It is always about what is right.

WHEN A MISTAKE IMPACTS YOUR CUSTOMERS, MAKE IT RIGHT

How do you behave with friends or loved ones when you make mistakes? From time to time I make the mistake of being late to dinner with my wife. When I do, it hurts because that's a special hour that we block several times per week to enjoy each other's company. When I mess up, I overcompensate with flowers, chocolates, etc., and before long, even though she is upset, she knows that I care. Not because of the gifts, but because I genuinely treasure our time together and would do anything to make it right.

Oftentimes in business, there is no overcompensation. Traditionally, if someone has a complaint, the company responds according to the amount of money the customer spent. Now, I'm not suggesting that everyone has to be treated equally. I don't treat all of my family and friends equally either, but I do care about all of them, and it shows. This needs to be evident in a Peoplework business as well. In the people revolution, humility and transparency will be evident when you care for and about your customers.

Systemizing your Life/Business

Being human in business sounds great, but the challenge comes in with scale. The same way companies have scaled being non- human you can scale being human. The secret, however, is systems. Think about how you might implement a system to effectively track and manage the financial side of your business. Human companies implement systems

37

that enable them to be more human at scale. At dotloop, we do just that for companies in the real estate space. By removing obstacles like paperwork, people in the real estate business are able to deliver more human experiences, at scale, because of the dotloop system.

Regardless of the industry you serve, systems are the only way to scale a human company.

SYSTEMS ARE THE ONLY WAY TO SCALE A HUMAN COMPANY

A Peoplework company is constantly obsessed with scaling human processes. One very human experience that has caught many people's attention is the Apple Store experience. From the moment you walk in the store, you feel good. You are greeted by a helpful rep, and, after quickly finding what you need, you can touch and feel it in real-time. When you are ready to check out, it's a simple credit card swipe and the receipt is in your inbox before you walk out the door. What makes all of that possible with thousands of stores, tens of thousands of employees and millions of customers? Systems.

As a Realtor you could never scale helping more people buy or sell a home if you did not have as system like the Multiple Listing Service. It allows you to look at thousands of homes on a computer, so you can then show a handful of them to interested buyers.

Without the MLS (or something comparable, like a more accurate version of Zillow) in place, a real estate agent would actually work with significantly fewer people. You could physically drive around to research only so many homes compared to "logging on" and seeing an entire database at once. Systems are the only way to scale human interactions for a business.

Unlike most people who have a small circle of close friends or family members, many businesses serve hundreds or thousands (and in Apple's case, millions) of customers. Being a human business requires systems, because just a few people can't service the many. So as you go about scaling your human business, don't forget that certain systems or technology that may seem "non-human" on the surface may very well be necessary to be a human company at scale.

At the end of the day, people connect with human companies, not robotic ones. So let it become part of who you are as a company. Encourage your employees to think this way too. Lead by example, and make it known what being a human company means. You don't have to be perfect, and, believe it or not, your customers don't expect perfection. Even Apple screws up sometimes. It's not going to be what you do or who you are that changes, it's going to be how you embrace it when serving your customers. Being human is as important as building good products or delivering quality work, so make sure you block the time to be human.

Wrong Goals

The goals of most businesses today do not involve a human component. Or if they do, the goals are all wrong. For example, when on a phone call with a friend, is your goal to minimize the time on the call or to get the most from that conversation? Most businesses with call centers focus on minimizing the time per call, not maximizing the value of each conversation. If the goal with all of your friends was to have the shortest calls possible, how long would you be friends? What if you forwarded your wife's calls to a guy halfway around the globe who didn't speak her language fluently? Flip your current thought process on its head and, as Apple taught us, think differently. Does your business care and does it show? Do your personal and business morals and ethics align?

People think about business the way we were trained to think about business. However, if you approached your business the way you approached your friends and family, things would be different.

My co-author Chris Smith, along with his business partner Jimmy Mackin, launched a real estate digital marketing company called Curaytor in January 2013. By October 2013 they had exceeded their goals for the year by 125%. However, they decided to temporarily hit the pause button and stop adding new customers, even with demand hitting an all-time high. Although this action appeared counterintuitive to growing a start-up company, and would most certainly not thrill an investor, Chris and Jimmy's goal was to focus their undivided attention on existing customers in order to provide a better product and service. This allowed them to rebuild their infrastructure, and in turn helped grow their business even more when they started taking in new customers again. Most importantly, their customers felt like family when they heard the news!

In the Peoplework era, companies will see the big picture and realize, just as Chris did, that quality, not just quantity, is what matters in personal relationships AND in business. When you focus on the human aspects of your company, you will win.

QUALITY, NOT JUST QUANTITY, IS WHAT MATTERS IN PERSONAL RELATIONSHIPS AND BUSINESS

Businesses Built like Relationships

In business, you can have millions of customers, each built over time. A business that is personal actually scales better than a business that is impersonal. The digital revolution enabled this new reach and for the first time, humanity can be scaled to an infinite degree.

Social media, mobile apps, blogs and YouTube can connect us like a human before they connect us like a business. However, building relationships that stay connected takes time. So, how can a human business generate revenue in month one or two if real-world human relationships, like being someone's best friend, as an example, take time to develop? The answer is simple: you hustle. If you needed a job to feed your family, you wouldn't wait for it to fall into your lap, right? You would use every bit of energy and resource available to make sure you didn't let them down. Use that sense of urgency and focus when becoming a Peoplework and human company. "Currency" with family and friends is time; with business it's money. Money is a by-product of human activities. We can help you work smarter in the people revolution, but working harder will be up to you. Thinking about your business differently is the first step.

The Seven Core Pillars

So if you agree on the foundation of what makes people like other people, then it becomes obvious that the same concepts applied to business will also work. We like to call these concepts the Seven Core Pillars to being a human company. They are:

1. You must think about your business like a person who lives, breathes and evolves. Apply your own personality.

2. You must be genuine and transparent.

3. You must establish genuine human principles and core values.

4. You must care, and show it, every chance you get.

5. You must invest in change and systems to improve.

6. You must intertwine the principles and values that you embrace into every inch of your company's fabric.

7. You must manifest these new human company principles using palpable things like Mission Statements, Code of Ethics and Employee workbooks.

When you approach your business this way, your friends (clients) and employees (family) will behave this way too.

So, how do you scale an organization of thousands into being more human? The short answer is, you apply the seven core pillars with a focus on systems, processes and specialization of task.

In the real world, this manifests at the highest level as the following:

Own an Apple product? Yes.
Have a great experience? Yes.

Let's use Apple products as an example and ask yourself this question: Why do Apple products have such a strong appeal to people?

1. Apple is who it is just like a normal human being. It does not try to be like any other product.

2. Apple scaled humanity through processes, systems and specialization of tasks (i.e., Apple Care, Retail Experience, Genius Bar)

Apple is one of those Peoplework companies that has shown that bein_ a human company creates a viral effect when done right. It created the outbreak and others have followed in their attempts to infect the populous. It all started by simply being a human company infused with passion. Let Apple be your proof; let your own individual personality be your passion. There's no better time to start running a human business than now!

*****

CASE STUDIES

HUMAN COM PANIES IN ACTION

Toms

Toms is a California-based company that designs and sells shoes, as well as eyewear. Creator and owner Blake Mycoskie first got the design idea for his shoes from an Argentine alpargata design. Mycoskie was first drawn to the country of Argentina while competing on the "Amazing Race" with his sister in 2002. Later, when he vacationed there in 2006, he became intrigued by the canvas slip-on shoes, alpargatas, worn by the local polo players. These shoes later became the inspiration for the classic Toms shoes. On that same trip, he noticed that many children were barefoot. Mycoskie learned that the lack of shoes threatened their ability to attend school and posed a threat of serious infection.

After discovering that Argentina had a larger shoelessness problem than other developing countries, Mycoskie decided that he wanted to develop a shoe like the alpargata for the North American market. The caveat was that for every shoe sold in North America, Toms would donate a shoe to a child in need.

He took his idea to Argentinian shoe manufacturers and initially made 250 pairs of shoes to sell in 2006. An article in the LA Times led to an online order that was nine times the available stock. As a result, 10,000 pairs of Toms were sold in the first six months and 10,000 children who needed them got a pair of shoes.

Mycoskie's business model has been described as "expressly built for purpose maximization" and "caring capitalism." Toms is selling both shoes and its ideals. Customers are able not only to buy shoes for themselves, but also become benefactors to someone they've never met. Toms Shoes is a human company that is winning. [v]

Zappos

Zappos.com is an online shoe and apparel shop founded in 1999. It has since grown, becoming the largest online shoe store. Nick Swinmurn, founder of Zappos, was first inspired when he failed to find a particular pair of shoes at his local mall. He later approached venture capitalists Tony Hsieh and Alfred Lin with the idea of selling shoes online. Although there was some initial skepticism, with $2 million the company was officially launched. Zappos, a variant of the Spanish word for shoes, "zapatos," uses a business model based on relationship marketing and loyalty. Word of mouth and repeat buyers helped the company surpass its goals of $1 billion in sales in 2010. The company has also built a positive customer service reputation by offering free shipping and free returns on all orders. Zappos now sells clothing and accessories, as well as a large variety of shoes.

With a company built on customer service, Zappos employees do not have limits on call times and do not work from scripts. They are also empowered to offer free upgrades to overnight shipping for loyal or even first-time customers. This is Peoplework in practice — emphasizing company culture and core values.

"If we get the culture right, then everything else, including the customer service, will fall into place," says Hsieh when discussing Zappos' approach to its customers.

There are countless other places to buy shoes online, but Zappos is a human company that is winning using a very simple strategy: caring the most. [vi]

Principle 3

CHANGE REQUIRES A BLUEPRINT

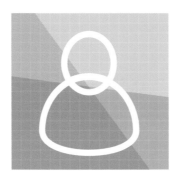

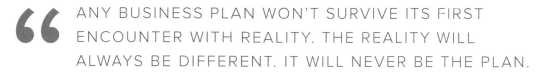 ANY BUSINESS PLAN WON'T SURVIVE ITS FIRST
ENCOUNTER WITH REALITY. THE REALITY WILL
ALWAYS BE DIFFERENT. IT WILL NEVER BE THE PLAN.

-JEFF BEZOS

The last ten years, during the peak (and tail end) of the digital revolution, we had two clear choices when it came to change. Change and grow, or don't and die. In a Peoplework business, change is not a yes or no, it is a yes and how. Change during the people revolution is just as important as finance, marketing, product and sales. Most companies don't treat change, or even view it, as being truly important to their bottom line, especially when compared to the others. Once you plan for change, and manage it effectively, your business will prosper.

Change is no longer optional because the world moves too fast. Businesses must grab change by the horns, because in the people revolution, change is officially normal. In fact, it is so normal that it can be disruptive if you do not know how to plan for it.

CHANGE IS NO LONGER OPTIONAL BECAUSE THE WORLD MOVES TOO FAST

Change Has A Blueprint

The first thing to understand about change in the Peoplework era is that there has been a fundamental shift in the impact, frequency and importance of change. Companies have not only bought into all things digital, they have invested everything they have into it. Massive digital changes can be seen all around us. For example, Google is changing the game regarding Internet connection speeds with its Google Fiber initiative. Today's lightning-fast Wi-Fi and LTE will soon feel like a dial-up modem once did. Tesla, and its game-changing electric cars, will have free power stations throughout the U.S. in a few years, not decades. [vii] Can you wrap your mind around never pumping or using gas again? By the time you read this book, we may all have an Apple iWatch on our wrists. Amazon is currently building massive warehouses that will offer most of the United States same-day shipping from its seemingly endless catalog of products. [viii] eBay will now deliver almost anything to your door within an hour of ordering if you live in San Francisco or New York City. Overnight delivery will soon change and same-day delivery will be the new normal and expected experience.

The last time you bought a home it likely involved piles of paper and miscommunication all the way up to the closing table. The next time you buy one, you'll be touching a tablet at Starbucks, thanks to companies like ours (dotloop).

Change, in a Peoplework company, is much like technology. It should be used as an enabler to work better with people. Peoplework businesses plan for change and bake it into their corporate strategy. Literally, they spend as much time planning for change as they do for growing sales. They give change a blueprint.

How Do You Make Change Happen?

Start by understanding the psychology of change. With change, people generally fall into one of three buckets. One-third embrace change (early adopters), a second third swing with the masses (majority/tipping point/most important) and the remaining third will kick and scream, no matter what (laggards). So check off the early adopter box, and then focus on the majority. They are the only two buckets that make the difference. It is a no-win, uphill battle at best to get the kickers and screamers to buy in, so don't pour all of your energy into trying. Eventually they won't have a choice.

As a society, we've come to expect change; we are at least to some degree comfortable with it. In the people revolution, change is on steroids; it is happening faster and deeper than ever before. The amount of revenue a company like Apple generates from products that didn't even exist a year ago is staggering. Facebook went from an idea in a dorm room to connecting one in seven people around the planet in no time. This exponential opportunity for scale and growth means that businesses must do more than just change, they must be excited by it! Change is like technology — it moves quickly.

PEOPLE NEED TO BE MOTIVATED TO CHANGE

People need to be motivated to change by someone or something prodding them along the path. It took me six months to switch my web browser from Internet Explorer to Google Chrome. The actual effort it took to change my browser? One click. The delay was nothing more than my own resistance to change. I wasn't ready to invest the five minutes it would take to reset all of my bookmarks and passwords until I was forced.

I often hate upgrading to the new look of Gmail or installing the latest version of WordPress. It took me what felt like forever to change from Outlook to Gmail. Just as I started to enjoy using it, I started instead checking my emails on my phone much like on a laptop in a browser. There was a day about a decade ago when you probably thought owning a cell phone, which would allow anyone to call you at any time, was invasive and unappealing. Now you sleep with it.

Remember, we also thought not too long ago that a physical keyboard on a smartphone was a must? BlackBerry thought the same thing and didn't blueprint change while meeting the demands of the moment. Instead, they relied on the status quo and got leapfrogged by innovation. Apple and Google, companies with cultures built on change, crushed them.

We even change and then change back. Change takes time and energy (dip and lag). The fifteen-minute dip and then three-day/ one week/three month long learning curve is too much to make a change even if we know it would make our lives easier. Businesses need to understand this because it can be destructive. If Chrome were more than a few clicks to install, it would not have become my new browser. Recognize there is and will continue to be a demand for "frictionlessness" and "instant" change. It will save you a lot of headaches and make getting any type of initiative adopted faster by removing all barriers to entry.

Grab A Mirror

Start changing by focusing internally first. Most companies change the way they think their customers want or need them to change. Before a business starts thinking about changing for their customers, they have to start changing internally. This begins with the company's leadership team.

Change trickles down, not up. As the CEO of dotloop, how I personally change, and how I drive change internally, will determine the success of our company in the people revolution. At one point, sales were likely the top priority for many CEOs like myself. Then it becomes things like growing the company, hiring talent, product development and HR. Change is never a focus. Change doesn't get its own meetings or VP. However, at a Peoplework company it does.

A good example of how we implement change is a weekly call between Chris and me dedicated to change. We meet for thirty minutes every Friday, without fail, to simply talk about what needs to change at dotloop. These change meetings impact every department and operational process, especially over time — just like exercising does for your body.

Beyond that weekly call, we also have a Culture Coach at dotloop who spends time managing change internally. He talks to Loopers, gauges how change is being received and ultimately develops a blueprint for change that evolves over time.

Like Peoplework, change is not something that you spend a lot of time learning about in school. And since change is changing, it's not easy to keep up. So plan to learn if you want to be a great leader of change. And it starts with books just like this one.

A frequently overlooked best practice is regularly reading new things. Books, search engines, blogs and social media channels provide more access to information than has previously been available in the history of mankind. In a people revolution, businesses must continually be learning their craft — sharpening their axe.

Attend industry specific leadership conferences in person. Don't just send your Marketing and IT people; spend time at the booth belly-to-belly with your customers and potential customers. Surround yourself with mentors and advisors who value change. Have a purpose while changing so that you know what direction you are heading at all times.

Not Everyone Changes The Same

In order to change, you must be able to embrace change and accept the need for it. However, not everyone embraces change in the same way. Oftentimes, younger people change faster, or can be trained to do so more quickly. Why? They are earlier in their careers and, demographically, they grew up with change. Living at the end of the digital revolution, as opposed to the beginning, created a large gap in the generations, "digital natives" versus "digital immigrants." Though our youth are the most familiar with the digital age, change still is not easy.

The more established someone is in their career, the more they will have to work to change. For example, a fifty-eight-year-old Realtor with thirty-five years of experience will take longer to change than a second-year Realtor in their twenties. Being more seasoned could mean you need to spend up to half of your time on change. There's nothing wrong with this, it's just a by-product of the amount of time spent in different environments by different groups of people. Just because A plus B equaled C for the last thirty-five years does not mean it will be a good indicator of future success. Remember, this is a revolution. Just ask the following industries: Newspaper, Television, Music, Travel, and Book Publishing.

The takeaway from this is that, in the people revolution, you must forget about what worked in the past and propel yourself to change with the future. Live in the moment and plan for tomorrow.

Youth Are Not Immune To Change

I think a majority would agree that what young people are taught in school does not necessarily translate into what they need to know in the real world. No one educates on change, but it is one of the core pillars of any successful business in the Peoplework era.

In the start-up world, where people and companies work fast and change frequently, oftentimes the changes happen too late. Whether it's removing an employee who's not a good fit or adjusting a product to meet customers' needs, change generally can't happen too fast. Beyond speed though, the real differentiator is not when but how the change happens. The most successful Peoplework business plan is change.

Then, when your blueprint for change changes, you adjust and plan for the next change. Be ready, the chess pieces will get shuffled around regularly, and this can get uncomfortable, even for young people.

We used to (and still do sometimes) think about fancy job titles and moving up the ladder as primary goals. That is dysfunctional and inefficient in the Peoplework era. Don't worry about whether someone else is climbing the ladder faster than you are. Ladder progression only happens in a Peoplework organization because it is needed to support the change that is required in the business. Change is about doing what you need to do in the moment, then preparing to be ready for what you need to do next to grow your business.

Core Values And Change

Beyond yourself and the people you surround yourself with, young and old, culture management takes hard work. Beware that change, when improperly managed, can be a drain on culture. If you kill a culture you can kill a company, which is why you should always manage change with a core set of company values in mind. Values set the expectations, and define the rules. Managing a company culture in an environment of constant change is about being willing to draw a line in the sand. Just remember it is sand, not concrete.

Businesses evaluate sales and marketing daily, weekly, monthly and quarterly, but they never evaluate how they are dealing with change. If change isn't incorporated into your values, it should be. Stating core values in an employee handbook is not enough; you have to reinforce your core values daily. Write them on the walls and in the cubicles. Force meetings that discuss the company's core values, and focus on change and culture. Talk about new people moving into the organization, but also about people choosing to leave, and provide open information about both. Talk about firing people and how the decision aligned with the company's core values. When managed properly, change should not be scary. Make sure any change is communicated openly across the organization and everyone is knowledgeable about what is happening and why. A Peoplework company embraces change, and is willing to grow.

As people change and grow, their company should highlight those efforts. It's the little things that matter, so make sure you create a system to make the little things happen. At dotloop, we have a culture committee and we often highlight the people who best embody our core values. It never feels perfect, but thinking about it and paying attention to the little things adds up. Change will take a lot of time and attention, as you might expect. Nonetheless, it is worthwhile for a Peoplework company.

Crowdsourcing Change

After your internal business is buttoned up, then you start focusing outward. Start by understanding your customers' needs and how those will change more frequently than ever. A few practical things you can do immediately that are "people facing" include:

- Crowdsource customer feedback from social media as often as you can. Ask for comments or likes as the litmus test on changes. Be candid and genuine and don't only show up twice a year.

- Set up "listening devices" with keywords from your specific niche. Tools like Google Alerts, Mention and Hootsuite make this easy and free.

- Send customer surveys by email using a free service like Survey Monkey.

- Do A/B testing on your website, in your email marketing and lead response campaigns, as well as with your social media strategy and content strategies.

The goal is to listen so that you know what your customers want. Only then are you truly ready to change. Then, plan to evolve, or change, your product constantly, whatever that may be. This must be ongoing. It used to be normal to push a new software update every six months. Now, post digital revolution, many companies push updates every couple of weeks, or even daily. Why? Because regular change makes it normal, efficient, and if done right, it's faster and less disruptive than not having constant change.

In contrast, Apple does not change based solely on customer feedback. They never supported Flash even when millions of their users were begging for it and publicly complaining. Why? Steve Jobs couldn't put a dent in the universe with Flash. He knew that, but his customers didn't. Trust your customers, but also trust your people and your intuition. Like many things, change is a combination of art and science.

Putting Change Into A Plan

Every change needs a plan and that plan must be managed. You want change to happen over a period of time and not too abruptly, so, the impact of every change should be considered. In addition, change should be modeled and generally tested on a small audience that gets progressively larger over time. Getting customers engaged in the process is also key. You can do this by building up real-time communication channels with top users, most influential users, and yes, most annoying users.

From time to time, evolution is not enough, and you need to innovate. Yahoo and AOL are good examples of implementing this recently. Knowing "cool" was out of reach, they have both turned to acquiring "cool" instead. Tumblr and Huffington Post are much more hip than "You've Got Mail" is right now. But of course that will change soon too. Often the hottest websites today are gone tomorrow. Just ask MySpace! Change is evolution at its finest.

Think of initiated change as the difference between innovation and evolution. Evolution will occur naturally, but from time to time you need to innovate to get ahead and stay there.

Innovation requires precision and planning. You can't expect change to just happen, or to be able to use someone else's blueprint for change. The best plan for change includes: a clear vision for the long-term goal, timing for changes rolling out, expected milestones along the change path, hard dates to evaluate change progress, a detailed report (company-wide) noting success (or failure) of change initiatives and monitoring the progress along the way. We did mention change was not easy. Most businesses don't have a "change department." Change requires its own plan; it requires dedicated staffing and accountability at the executive and field levels to work.

Part of managing change effectively is not just creating a blueprint, but meeting regularly to change as needed. Make change an intricate part of your strategy. Have quarterly strategy meetings focused on change, evaluate the progress of change, evaluate the change plan, and most importantly change as needed. Change is not easy, but it can be exciting. Change must be treated as important as the other parts of your business.

Don't underestimate the power of changing. It can make or break your business. A Peoplework company sees change as mission critical — on the same level as finance, marketing, product and sales. Once you plan for change and manage it effectively, your business will prosper. The upside of change is that your customers and employees are already waiting for it!

CASE STUDIES

CHANGE IN ACTION

Meg Whitman

Former eBay chief executive and current Hewlett-Packard chief executive Meg Whitman knows that in any business change is essential as a means to survival. Her understanding of change began 26 years ago when she was a junior partner working for Tom Tierney at Bain & Company. Walking into his office one day, she asked if he wanted staff feedback about his leadership style. He allowed it and heard this junior partner tell him he was domineering and didn't allow his staff to step up in their leadership role.

Though initially stunned, Tierney soon warmed up to Whitman's feedback and toned down his harshness. As a result, the entire Bain company benefited. It took guts for Whitman to walk into that room and deliver those words to Tierney, but it resulted in increased respect.

In 2011, Whitman became CEO at HP, where stock had been tanking and operating margins shrinking. Months later, HP lost out, again, to archrival Dell on a big server order from Microsoft's Bing search engine team.

This loss pushed Whitman into action. She immediately phoned Microsoft's CEO and asked where her company came up short. CEO Steve Ballmer sent Whitman a multipage memo outlining ways HP dropped the ball on this missed opportunity.

Whitman got busy appointing teams of people to help improve the company — from computing to operations to supply. She made it their mission to figure out how to make HP more competitive by implementing cost-saving steps, fixing software bugs and developing a more customer-friendly approach. It paid off! A year later, HP won that Bing contract.

Meg Whitman is a team builder who understands how to rally the troops together to accomplish a goal, without being afraid of the work that needs to be done. This is what makes her one of the best CEOs on the planet.

When Whitman first started at HP, her goal was to fix what they had. She started by overhauling how the company sells and determining if it was helping to retain customers. Although she knew she was competing with the likes of Google, Facebook and Dropbox, who were providing customers with opportunities to share their documents and photos ink-free, Whitman didn't want to give up on the fact that corporations still bought printers.

Whitman also made herself available by having more than three hundred one-on-one meetings with customers or sales-channel partners and small groups, in an effort to better appeal to customers and increase sales. "Make it Matter" became Whitman's brand messaging motto.

Whitman is beyond financial motivation, it's about making a legacy. [ix]

JC Penney

JC Penney in 2011 appointed Ron Johnson as CEO to save the struggling retail company. He lasted only seventeen months and made many mistakes.

Johnson was tasked with improving and updating the JC Penney Brand. After all, Johnson had been able to turn the Apple Store into a monster success story when he worked there, so surely he could do it for JC Penney. However, his plans for JC Penney were too bold.

The blueprint for one company did not work for the other. Essentially, Johnson was ousted because of his epic failure.

In early 2012, Johnson announced a new "fair and square" everyday low pricing scheme and did away with sales and coupons. This plan backfired.

It didn't take long for people to note that Johnson's no- coupons, no-sales experiment was failing to attract shoppers. JC Penney later dropped this experiment and chose to focus on making JC Penney a hip "destination" shopping experience. However, most of the company's loyal customers felt like they were no longer JC Penney's target market.

This was an example of mismanaged change that turned destructive. Essentially, Johnson did not get to know his customer base and ended up misreading what shoppers really wanted. He didn't test his ideas in advance, and as a result, he alienated his core customers. [x]

Principle 4

PURPOSE BEFORE TECHNOLOGY

 EFFORTS AND COURAGE ARE NOT ENOUGH WITHOUT PURPOSE AND DIRECTION.

-JOHN F. KENNEDY

For centuries, human beings have responded better to instant gratification than delayed. After all, why wouldn't we respond better to faster gratification when gratification feels good? But things can't always be instant. Did your mother ever tell you great things might be worth waiting for? The digital revolution greatly exaggerated our demand for instant gratification, because instant access became the rule, and not the exception. Since things move faster, shiny and fast is more prevalent now than it has ever been. And in many ways, we've become spoiled, expecting that relief and satisfaction should always happen in the here and now. As a result, we run the risk of favoring immediate results over the true purpose of whatever it is that we are doing. Said differently, we put technology before purpose.

In the Peoplework era, it's more important than ever that purpose is at the heart of every decision or investment you make in your business. It comes before technology, it comes before finance, it is the reason that we do what we do. Have you written your purpose as a business lately? If you start with purpose you will end up with technology that truly matters. When you put purpose before technology, you will get purpose-driven results.

The Digital Revolution did a lot of really positive things for us as a society and business community, but it also introduced a number of distractions. Day after day our inbox fills up with what everyone else thinks we should spend our time on. The hard part is figuring out where YOU think you should be spending your time (hint: start with your purpose). Although we now have the ability to digitally connect with almost anyone through social media, as well as get our emails and text messages instantly, we often are no longer focusing on who is right in front of us! The good news is that new digital technologies will also kill this digital overload.

In the financial world this phenomenon manifests itself in the form of a day trader, who trades stocks on a daily basis. Think about that for a moment, why would anyone in his or her right mind buy and sell a company in the same day as the norm? All of these trades eventually will become automated, with an algorithm more successful than the trader ever was, and thus digital will destroy digital. Both good and bad have come from this short-term mindset. The good is that we are more urgent, with higher expectations. However, as expectations climb higher and higher, the urgency to react becomes exaggerated. The bad thing is that the same impulses, coupled with this microwave mentality, can lead to bad decision making if the right controls are not put in place. The ultimate control is having a clear understanding of your purpose, and using that as the guiding foundation for every decision that you make in your life or business. When you lead with purpose it provides focus, not a need to only get quick results.

Be Urgent About The Right Things

Putting purpose first doesn't mean that you can't or shouldn't be urgent, because urgency and purpose are not mutually exclusive. Sometimes speed seems more important than purpose, but urgency is what sells, not speed.

Leading with purpose doesn't mean you're not urgent, it just means you're urgent about the right things. For example, data has shown that as many as 70% of web leads in business come from simply choosing the first person they speak with. This isn't because you are picking up the phone quickly. It's because the opportunities created from this urgency are powerful and limitless, but you have to marry that with being purposeful about what type of customers you speak with. Using the "lead to answer response time" example as one reason why you want to be urgent, it's understandable why purposeful urgency is critical. Without it, you'll lose business. The risk, of course, is that we become too urgent in response to opportunity and lose sight of the bigger picture — your customers. Technology only enables the speed to contact. Being a person in a digitally connected world is why they called with the urgency needed to close them in the first place.

We saw this phenomenon when the mobile app ecosystem first surfaced. According to a study done by Pinch Media, "The vast majority of apps downloaded from the App Store are in use by less than 5% of users after one month has passed since the download." I'm sure there are many studies just like it that would support that we download a lot of shiny objects that never get used. In the Peoplework era, don't start by downloading an app, instead, start by identifying a problem.

Oftentimes in business, features, function and technology are placed ahead of purpose. You'll see this when companies market that their features and functions will make your life better. But companies that focus on the purpose behind their business never market features. They don't have to. Amazon never marketed features, but instead focused on simplifying shopping, and, similarly, PayPal wanted to make online transactions simple. A Peoplework company understands that it must have purpose behind its business in order to remain committed to their customers, and their profits.

Reason Behind Purpose

Let's take a few steps back for a moment. Generally, purpose always has a motive behind it. There is a reason for choosing to do something and doing it. Let's say you go to the store to buy a drill. You have in mind only one purpose for that drill — to make a hole in a wall, for example. But we often lose sight of this initial purpose and end up with drills that are able to do more than what we needed them to do. Or in my case, I always got suckered into the entire toolkit in the fancy bag with a flashlight and extra batteries. The problem is that we think "tool," not purpose. We get attracted to shiny objects and we lose sight of our true purpose. It's easy to do.

Imagine the outcome if you had remained focused on the initial purpose. Maybe there were better, more cost-effective ways to get the hole drilled. Maybe you didn't need the entire tool kit that comes with a circular saw, two extra-strength batteries and a flashlight that you'll never use. Or if you did just buy a drill, maybe you didn't need to spend the extra hundred dollars on features and functionality designed for professional contractors.

This happens all of the time in our industry. Real estate is a very competitive business. Brands generally compete to keep up with the Joneses (i.e., at parity with the others) and to be different (creating a competitive advantage). Over the last five years, a company's online web presence has been a big part of that attempt at differentiation. As a result, we have seen a massive phenomenon of focus around new websites, mobile apps, video marketing, etc. When consumers started going online in masses to find homes, it was easy for a broker owner to think "it's time to get a new website." Millions of dollars were spent on websites, leads, videos, QR codes and whole host of other technologies that may not have fully addressed their core purpose. Instead of keeping up with the Joneses, or focusing on being different, sometimes the best question to ask is "What exactly are we trying to accomplish and why are our agents saying that?" If the answer to that question is "deliver the best customer experience, regardless of what the competitors are doing," you will win. What you focus on will determine your purpose.

Businesses often think that technology solves problems, but it doesn't. Technology can, and in many cases should, be part of the solution, but you can't start there. Take a real estate website for example. The investment in a new real estate website, and why the agent even brings it up to their broker in the first place, is likely because they simply want to look good in front of their clients. They want other people to like them, and to trust them. If a certain percentage of their clients interact with them online, that first and ongoing impression is key. When it comes to real estate, a homebuyer wants to buy a home, not become a lead and go through your "sales funnel." So, one purpose might be to make agents and clients feel good. Going deeper, you should ask, "Why do they go online?" Most likely to search for properties. They may also want to learn more about why they should pick John Doe of ABC Real Estate versus another person or company. Assuming that those reasons are comprehensive, a broader purpose might be to provide clients with resources online so they can always find what they need quickly. The end solution might very well be a new website, but when you start with the purpose and understand it deeply, you go down an entirely different and more purposeful path. Most importantly, you will end up doing a better job helping your clients do what they need to do, quickly and effectively. And there you have it — technology just enabled the purpose to be achieved.

Purpose-First Approach

When you establish an objective, only then does what you are trying to accomplish become clear. But, sadly, a purpose-first approach is not the norm. The norm is to find a new website provider first so that they can tell you about all of the features and functions they offer. This approach ends with you implementing lots of bells and whistles that no one even uses. Think of it like the entire toolkit when all you'll ever use or need is the drill. You end up with a website that is more about what you or your website provider thought you needed versus what your clients actually needed. Now, the website is probably not a total failure, the technology-first approach has worked for you in the past. Nonetheless, the greater opportunity here is to satisfy the needs of your client. That only happens when you put people and purpose first. In a people revolution, you first examine your purpose before resolving with technology. Purpose is your guiding light to solutions.

So, if we can all agree that putting purpose before technology makes sense, let me be clear that it's easier said than done. However, it is not impossible. There are three actions for putting purpose first:

1. Gain Understanding

2. Establish Priorities

3. Focus on Simplicity

Gain Understanding

Gaining clarity about what it is that you want to achieve is the first step. Most of us focus on the technologies, because that is what the marketplace wants us to do. Marketing of the past was about telling you what you needed. For example, if you want to finish something on time, you are told that new systems or the latest five-star mobile app is the answer. Looking for a better way to track your to-do lists? We are told that systems or apps will help you there. And it is the same story if you need help finding things you've lost or a better way to manage your money.

There is no shortage of tools, and technically you could implement them all. But you'll end up not using half of them because you don't understand how to incorporate them effectively in your life and business.

What if you had broader clarity on what it is that you are trying to accomplish? For example: "I want to be a productive and balanced person by spending the right amount of time on the things that matter to me. I also want to keep track of what is going on as efficiently as possible." From there, you would storyboard what this looks like: Every day I wake up, and I see what I need to do for that day. Then, I open up my calendar and each of those items is listed. As I work, I am notified when I am out of time and given the choice to move onto the next thing or to stop where I am and have that carry over to the next day.

Whatever that storyboard looks like, it will be your roadmap. With a roadmap in hand, you can then begin to evaluate what technologies help to enable that purpose. Once you know the purpose you must prioritize the action.

Establish Priorities

Most of us manage our lives in a very task-oriented way. We think about every day very much like our bucket list for life. I need to get XYZ done today. We just want to check the finish box, which is why it's easy to turn to technology first — the illusion of simplicity. When you think about the reasons why we do the things we do, you will discover that most of them do not make a lot of sense. Just doing things to check the box doesn't necessarily mean progress or desired results. Establishing priorities is about focusing on long-term productivity, not short-term actions. True balance and productivity are achieved by spending the right amount of time on the things that matter most to you or your business. The same secret applies to life. Spending time on the right things is the secret to productivity.

Let's say that you set an internal date to have a website for your business published. There are very real implications associated with that goal, like customer expectations, design deadlines and other dependencies out of your control. But, at its root, the website is only there to enable your greater purpose. So you should not focus on hitting a date just to check a box. Instead, the only box that should be your priority to check is the one that says, "I have fulfilled my purpose." That is the only thing that matters.

When every minute of your day is mapped back to your purpose, prioritized in order of impact and importance, you will achieve your purpose, the only checkbox that matters.

Focus On Simplicity

In our business at dotloop, I can't count the number of real estate brokers who say, "I want to be paperless." Paperless, as it is generally understood, is about dealing with less paper. The common "paperless" user story in real estate goes something like this: The buyer wants to purchase a home. The real estate agent prepares a lot of paperwork, which is then sent to the buyer. Lots of back and forth occurs. Finally, the paperwork is ready to be sent to the sellers, via email or fax. Then, the sellers change or adjust the paperwork. That entire process goes back and forth a number of times, negotiating and clarifying business terms. Finally, the parties agree to the terms. Then someone on the agent's staff, or possibly the agent themselves, scans the paper into an electronic format. Those electronic formats are then uploaded to the "paperless" system for storage and compliance. Sounds terrible right? That's why we always remind brokers and agents that being "paperless" is not the end game. That's not what clients want. Simply digitizing the paper process, as it existed in the past, isn't enough. What people really want is an easier way to work with one another, seamlessly online. Our digital paper should just be a by-product of Peoplework, not the other way around.

There is certainly some efficiency gained by having the final paperwork in electronic format. It is easier to manage, reduces storage costs and certainly lowers risk. The real issue, however, lies in the process. The problem is not, "How do I lessen the paper load?" Rather, it is, "How do I run a better business?" In the business of real estate, only one thing sells homes — people working with other people. So, it makes you wonder, why then do so many companies call us and say they want to be paperless? It's because everyone is doing it, and because they believe that bringing paper online will save money and time. Going "paperless" is like buying a car without seats and with a one-gallon gas tank. It will get you further than you can go without it, but it is not going to take you nearly far enough. Plus, even that short ride won't be comfortable and you'd be missing the entire purpose of an automobile — having the freedom to go where you need to go, when you want to, conveniently and comfortably.

The purpose of being in the real estate business is to help buyers and sellers find the home of their dreams, while delivering an amazingly valuable and professional experience — it's about people, not paper.

Real estate is not alone. We're all in the people business, and it's safe to say that the end goal of most companies in the Peoplework era has something to do with people working better together.

This is essentially the end goal of most businesses — to be able to work better and enable their employees to do the same. We believe so strongly in this as a Peoplework business that we actually changed our tag line to deliberately say it is not about paperwork anymore; it is about Peoplework. Traditional marketing would tell us to say, "we are paperless" and here are the "10 reasons why we are better than the next guy." Instead, we want companies to focus in on their real purpose, not the technology. Paperwork is complex; Peoplework is not. Whatever your purpose is, make sure you are simplifying complexity. It is more important than ever that you start with purpose.

From Death And Taxes To Change And Purpose

Putting purpose before technology produces better results, period. It allows you to stay focused on the right things all of the time. It ensures that technology serves the purpose that it was intended to. Therefore, tools should only enable the purpose. So whether it is a drill or a software solution, make sure you start with a road map that ends in purpose.

Now that we are in the Peoplework era, starting with purpose is the only option if you want to win. Remember the "paperless" real estate broker? Just being paperless isn't purpose worthy, but helping people work better together is. Like real estate, most businesses have more to download with people than paper, so start by focusing there.

Although your overarching purpose should be consistent, how you define and support it each quarter will evolve. Purpose can change over time, but you can never lose sight of it. In the end, it is about how you connect better with your clients. And remember that Peoplework businesses always have a purpose that puts people first. So when in doubt, start there.

*****

CASE STUDIES

PURPOSE IN ACTION

ShotSpotter

Thanks to technology created by ShotSpotter, if you fire a gun in certain neighborhoods, you may find yourself surrounded by police in just a few minutes, even though no one dialed 911.

ShotSpotter, founded in 1995 by scientist Robert Showen, allows police to pinpoint exactly where a gun was fired through the use of deployed acoustic sensors that listen for the sound of gunfire in neighborhoods. Next, the sensors are matched with an analyzing software that pinpoints the location of the fired round, while filtering out other sounds. Trained police officers hear the sound, confirm that it's gunfire and then alert officers to the location.

The data from ShotSpotter has been extremely useful for law enforcement. In fact, the City of Milwaukee is one of 74 cities that use the system as a strategy for fighting crime. Milwaukee's police chief stated that he was not interested in this technology just for technology's sake. Rather, he wanted to ensure that it assisted them in accomplishing their mission of helping people live in a safe neighborhood to raise their children and pursue the American dream.

Milwaukee's police department has used ShotSpotter to catch several criminals after they've fired shots. ShotSpotter data is also able to help police recover shell casings from weapons and deliver forensic evidence in court.

ShotSpotter is not a success because it produces helpful data and technological results, but because it provides law enforcement officers with a better way to keep people safe. The company has seen great success thus far and has raised $62 million, to date, from investors. [xi]

Nest Thermostat

The mundane has now become chic thanks to technology and design, with a whole new look for your basic thermostat. Founders Tony Fadell and Matt Rogers, both Apple alums, joined together to redesign the traditional thermostat. So in 2010, Nest was born.

Nest Labs (which was acquired in January 2014 by Google for $3.2 billion) designs and manufactures a Wi-Fi-enabled and programmable thermostat that learns from your manual adjustments. The main purpose of Nest is to analyze user behavior in heating and cooling for homes and businesses in order to minimize energy use.

While they were both working at Apple, Fadell and Rogers saw an opportunity in the market to give customers a better way to manage their energy consumption while also saving money. So, they raised approximately $50 million in startup money and released the Nest thermostat in October 2011.

The operating system built within Nest gives users the opportunity to interact with the thermostat by controlling a wheel of options on its menu. This menu allows users to access energy history, device settings, scheduling, and of course they are able to switch between heating and cooling. All of this is connected to the Internet, so users don't have to actually touch the screen on the thermostat. The Nest also includes a motion detector that turns up the heat or the air once someone gets home.

Nest went beyond the innovative thermostat to the sleek and smart smoke detector, released just this fall. Unlike other smoke detectors that let out a loud and annoying noise once smoke or carbon monoxide is located in the air, the Nest smoke detector alarms with a vocal warning that alerts owners that there is trouble. Nest believes that technology "should be about more than newest, loudest, prettiest. It should make a difference." They are working to provide their customers with a better overall experience. [xii]

Houzz

Want to get ideas on how to decorate your master bathroom, how to design your backyard to be more family friendly, or ask someone else how they did it? The best place to get all of these ideas is on the web in one location called Houzz.com.

Houzz is a web site and online community, founded in 2009, that features architecture, interior design and decorating, home improvement, landscape design and also articles from home design experts. Users are able to browse through numerous photos by rooms and style, and they are also able to upload photos of their own design or redesign projects to the site.

Co-founders Adi Tatarko and Alon Cohen were working on their own remodeling project when they got tired of cutting pages from magazines and adding them to their inspiration file. They quickly decided to create a database of photos online for people just like themselves who were in the middle of a home improvement or remodeling project. They wanted people to have an online service that provided them with ideas and support through the design process. Since its inception, Houzz has gained enormous popularity. In December 2012, the Houzz app was downloaded more than five million times and the website featured one million images.

Homeowners are also able to connect with the 1.5 million home improvement professionals on Houzz's website and its award-winning mobile apps. They are able to ask questions and get tips for design and improvement projects.

Houzz has been featured, with positive reviews, on news channels like CNN, and magazines like Real Simple, Architectural Digest, Bloomberg, Businessweek and TechCrunch. [xiii]

QUALITY CREATES QUANTITY

" QUALITY IS MORE IMPORTANT THAN QUANTITY. ONE HOME RUN IS MUCH BETTER THAN TWO DOUBLES.

-STEVE JOBS

It used to be that the best way to grow your business was by focusing on quantity, which meant more leads, more marketing, etc. The theory was simple: more leads = more sales. So we created more marketing tools, pushed more advertising and developed more leads, but through it all, we lost sight of the people. At one time, gaining access to leads was important because it did generate more business. Now, the notion of a lead no longer exists as it did in the past, because quantity has been commoditized and access to leads is without limit.

Focusing on quality, on the other hand, is the real opportunity in the Peoplework era. When you deliver quality experiences to your existing customers, they'll keep coming back and tell their friends about it too. In a Peoplework business, the new definition of a lead is a satisfied customer who then tells their friends about their experience. Imagine the value in having a customer for life. For example, when someone visits a restaurant and has a positive experience, they leave not only content from the meal, but also remembering their experience. If the experience was amazing, you can bet that they'll tell people about it. Whoever they tell will become a customer too, and then they tell their friends, and so on. This new opportunity to grow your business by focusing on quality is what Gary Vaynerchuk calls "Word of mouth, on steroids."

The most meaningful lead comes from a happy customer sharing information with others about a quality experience. Quality is contagious. Sustainable quantity over time means that you focus on quality.

It is easier to focus on quality during the people revolution largely because the influx of digital innovation increasingly makes people more rapidly accessible. Now that we are connected, the best way to grow is not more connections and leads, but more people-to-people interaction.

For this reason, in the Peoplework era it is actually quality that becomes as important, and eventually more important, than quantity.

Leads Are Overrated

During the digital era, we were trained to always want more leads, more likes, more followers, and more friends. That made sense because more connections equaled more business. Through connection, however, the key differentiator transitioned away from access to loyalty because once everyone had "access," it lost its value. Loyalty stems from quality not quantity. For example, Starbucks could buy customers through marketing ploys such as buy one, get one free coupons, Super Bowl commercials or by purchasing leads (advertising), and view each customer as just a cup of coffee that day. Instead, they think bigger than coffee, and focus on delivering the most amazing and consistent experience. Under the latter approach, every customer is a lifetime relationship.

EVERY CUSTOMER IS A LIFETIME RELATIONSHIP

For Starbucks, focusing on quality means going far beyond just coffee; their vision is to inspire and nurture the human spirit. And it's not just lip service; they mean it. In fact, there was a moment in Starbucks' history where the company lost the focus on quality that it was founded upon. So Howard Shultz, founder and then CEO, shut down every store in the country, because he recognized the need to refocus on quality. [xiv] Starbucks is a Peoplework business, and Peoplework businesses focus on quality customer generation and quality appointment generation, not lead generation. The quality of the connections that you establish with your customers is paramount. Loyalty = customers for life (they keep coming back) and virality (they tell their friends about it).

Less Is More

In the Peoplework era, you must start small in order to grow big. Building on the lead-generation theme, focusing on fewer leads sounds like a crazy idea, and it may very well be at first. However, in order to deliver quality at scale, you have to start small to master the quality experience. The first important concept to understand about quality is that less really is more. When you focus on fewer leads and deliver amazing experiences every time, few will become many over time. In a world where average doesn't cut it, even delivering reliably average experiences is now a losing business.

Delivering a quality experience on day one is paramount to the success of a business and the most proven and predictable way to create loyal customers. Loyalty isn't limited to coffee shops either. Whether you sell real estate, shoes or software, loyalty should be the goal. After all, we're all in the people business. For example, Evernote is a software product that I'm quite loyal to. Evernote has inverted the normal business model by focusing on quality first. Their initial download of the app is free. Once users download the app they have unlimited access to a set of Evernote services that make it easy to stay organized and productive while, despite being cost-free, still provide a great experience. During this time, their customers become more and more satisfied with their service. Why? It's because they focus on quality first and quantity second. You might be wondering where the quantity comes in. According to TechCrunch, Evernote users grow more valuable over time. New users of the app convert to the Premium package at a rate of .5% in the first thirty days. Though this number seems depressing by normal freemium standards, Evernote is showing just how the freemium model works. Of the Evernote users who signed up two years ago, most are still active and 20% have become paid customers. [xv] Impressed now? Focusing on quality first is a long-term strategy, but it's the only strategy that scales in a Peoplework world. In Evernote's case, a people-to-people interaction is a download of their app. For your business, it could be the customer's first visit to your website or the first time someone walks into your store.

In the Peoplework era, the goal is to deliver an amazing experience in order to give customers the most positive view of your company. Loyal customers = lifetime customers and lifetime customers = lifetime value.

Focusing only on quality is a business model practiced by some of the world's most successful companies but certainly not all. Some companies deliver a quality product but not a quality overall experience, and others do the opposite. This, in turn, creates a tremendous opportunity for the businesses that get it right. Apple is a great example. It is one of the most admired companies in customer experience, followed by some of the other greats like Amazon, Zappos, Starbucks and Disney. Apple focuses on just a few products, not a million, and obsesses over quality when traditional logic would suggest that quantity should be the focus. The quantity approach would mean more products, more features and more options. Focusing on quality, however, produces results, and Apple has the numbers to prove it: 88% of iPhone purchases in 2012 were made by repeat buyers, while 74% of iPad buyers were already Mac owners. Why do they see such high loyalty numbers? It might have something to do with the fact that a staggering 90% of Apple's customers reported being "extremely satisfied" with the service they received at the now famous Genius Bar.

A Peoplework company focuses on great experiences because they know it will produce loyal customers. Delivering the best experience goes beyond product design or quality, and extends to the expectations of your customers. Those expectations must be met or exceeded, every time.

Starbucks gets it. They meet or exceed our expectations consistently. Otherwise, you wouldn't have millions of people returning multiple times per week to pay $5.25 for a latte. Thanks to Starbucks we don't even think about coffee in the same way. Starbucks is an experience that has resulted in loyalty over time. Starbucks customers feel good from the moment they walk in the door. As they enter, they are greeted by an inviting and laid-back atmosphere where they can relax and enjoy a specialty coffee made just for them. It's about the experience, not just the coffee.

Oftentimes, companies get so caught up in quantity that they actually miss the big opportunity. Those companies need to switch from "funnel vision" to "tunnel vision."

SWITCH FROM "FUNNEL VISION" TO "TUNNEL VISION"

The Starbucks model works because they don't try to be everything to everyone. They brew a great cup of coffee and make you feel at home, but they target customers who are willing to pay for it. When you know your audience and focus on quality, each interaction is about more than that particular transaction; it's about a lifetime relationship. And the lifetime value of a customer is worth money — $14,000 in Starbucks' case. So whether your product is $4 or $4,000, quality creates lifetime relationships, and lifetime relationships mean repeat business. Think long-term. You won't have to buy leads when you deliver experiences that people love. We have entered an era where quality creates quantity.

The loyalty that Starbucks has achieved must not go unnoticed. So let's talk further about how exactly they create loyal customers and what it means to their bottom line.

When you hear Starbucks describe their experience as a break from the worries outside or a place where you can meet with friends, it sounds fluffy, right? It makes you wonder how that model works at $3–$5 per cup of coffee? It is called Lifetime Value of a Customer (LTV). Every time a customer walks in the door, Starbucks doesn't view the customer as a cup of coffee, but as a lifetime relationship and they understand, specifically, what a lifetime relationship means in the way of LTV.

Over the life of our relationship with Starbucks, we spend a fraction of what we will spend on a single real estate transaction. Yet, in the real estate industry, most agents and offices focus on leads, leads, and more leads. If lifetime value is of interest, which should be the case for any business in the Peoplework era, our focus should be on delivering amazing experiences, not more leads. The table below shows the breakdown of how the lifetime value of a Starbucks customer is calculated over time, and illustrates that a narrow focus creates big results.

Average spend per visit = $5.90

Average visits per week = 4.2 (value of $24.30 per week)

Average customer loyalty = 20 years

Average retention rate = 75% Profit Margin = 21.3%

Discount Rate = 10% for NPV (Net Present Value)

Gross Margin Averaged using 3 different

LTV models = $14,099 [xvi]

Apply this model to a larger transaction, like real estate, and imagine what the LTV might look like. Think about it: A $500,000 purchase versus a $5 cup of coffee. For fun, let's look at the same LTV model for a $300,000 real estate transaction:

Purchase Price of $300,000

3% commission = $9,000

Assumed you would get the buyer 50% of the time

Average sales per year = .02 (one every five years)

Average customer life = 30 years

Average retention = 75%

Profit Margin = 70% (30% to the broker)

Discount Rate = 10% for NPV (Net Present Value)

Gross Margin Averaged using 3 different
LTV models = $121,500

If you want to make $120,000 per year for the next thirty years, just get thirty of these customers. To go big you have to start small. In order to do this you must develop a completely different mindset. If the customer doesn't purchase right away, you still need to treat them like a lifetime customer and not like a lead. It's a long-term view. And the best news of all is that the LTV model doesn't even factor in the network effect.

The Network Effect

In the Peoplework era the "network of influence" has replaced the "circle of influence." The Internet made it easier and faster to establish trust. So if anyone can build trust, and anyone can buy leads, what does that leave you with? It means that you cannot just think about leads as numbers anymore, because that is not sustainable. Every "lead" is being sold multiple times, which means that the person on the other end is being bombarded by countless companies vying for their business. The only thing that will set you apart is experience.

THE ONLY THING THAT WILL SET YOU
APART IS EXPERIENCE

Once you focus on that, the network effect starts to work to your advantage. The number of Facebook friends that we have grew from one hundred to two hundred twenty-nine from 2008 to 2012. The average person now has fifty thousand friends of friends, and people have fifty percent more "close friends" online than offline.

Overwhelming? Yes. Discouraging? No. A networked world presents great opportunities if you're in the people business. Through it, people have a greater ability to share their positive experience with your company. Quality is about exceeding expectations. You are missing the boat if you're still focused on quantity instead of quality.

Every experience someone has with a company creates either a positive or a negative effect. It's no longer enough to be neutral as a company; you must always grow the satisfaction of your users and customers. Neutral means average and average means losing. The goal is to focus on quality in order to have lifetime customers.

Once you get people to understand that every single interaction can mean an increase in LTV, or a decrease in LTV, the light bulb turns on. A quality interaction can mean a direct increase in the LTV of a customer (quantity).

There is no shortage of data supporting that bad experiences travel fast. Reliably positive experiences are important because bad reviews travel rapidly. To cite one 2011 report from retailcustomerexperience. com, it is said that if someone has a good experience, they will more than likely tell nine people, but twice as many if they have a bad experience. A quality or amazing experience can have an even bigger impact because they will not only tell people, but they will also share the product with them, rave about it, promote it, and defend it. [xvii] Social media plays a large role in the success (and sometimes failure) of a company. In the Peoplework era, you have the opportunity to connect and stay connected with more people than ever before, and there are no excuses not to be; it's the new minimum standard, so take advantage of it.

Jeff Bezos, founder and CEO of Amazon.com, said it best when he stated, "If we can keep our competitors focused on us while we stay focused on the customer, ultimately we'll turn out all right." The quote speaks directly to quality. If we keep chasing the next customer and never focus on the one we already have, the overall experience suffers and then you have a real problem. As satisfaction level drops, loyalty drops at a faster rate.

Peoplework companies focus on all interactions, and not only the negative or problem-centric ones. They put the same amount of passion and purpose into all of them. So, how do you go about building a quality-centered business?

Step 1: Figure out who you want to be

You cannot be everything to everyone, so you must be willing to alienate and limit your audience. Whether your target market is rich or poor, male or female, you'd better know who they are and speak their language in order to achieve success. Measure their actual satisfaction, not by what they say, but what they do. In addition, you must be willing to walk away from customers or opportunities that don't fall within your target wheelhouse. That is a big part of knowing who you are. My wife is an interior decorator who wants to be only a modern, high-end, condo decorator. It means she should say no when she gets an inquiry that falls outside of that scope. The power of no is critical.

When you know who you are as a business, you know who your target market is, and you'll be positioned to deliver a better experience, consistently. Don't stray from it.

Step 2: Define the experience with the end user in mind

Focusing on the end user is not easy to do, it is just easy to say. Start thinking about leads as people and focus on quality first and foremost. Apple always starts with elegantly designed products. They believe simplicity is genius and constantly think differently. This is what a Peoplework company does.

The digital revolution created consumer expectations that do not come with an instruction-manual mindset. Historically, by taking a quality over quantity approach, Apple did not have to invest in advertising. Over time this has changed, but, even today, Apple spends half of what Microsoft does on advertising, yet it is twice the size. [xviii] This is a direct result of creating a quality product with the end user in mind.

Tony Hsieh, CEO of Zappos, is another example of a Peoplework leader who focuses on the end user. He's known for saying that Zappos is a "customer service company that happens to sell shoes." [xix] Zappos' secret sauce is its customer service AND its nearly endless selection of shoes by brand, color and size. Do not underestimate the power of convenience or the downside of friction. "Delivering happiness" would only go so far as a slogan if Zappos were out of my size every time I tried to use them.

Southwest Airlines could have used a lot more money to launch their company in 100 markets, but they chose to perfect their model in only five markets at first. [xx] They turned down quantity, focused on quality, and ended up creating quantity long-term.

A Peoplework company sets proper expectations that it knows it can deliver on, not empty promises that will result in failure.

Step 3: Deliver on the promise

Companies must continually meet, and ideally exceed, the expectations of their clientele in order to have lifetime customers. For example, buy something on Amazon and note the ultimate e-commerce experience. It's fast, easy, cheap, and delivers on the promise.

And, when possible, go beyond merely delivering on expectations to exceeding them. Zappos does "random acts of kindness" to exceed expectations, which includes things like free overnight shipping for first-time orders. Gary Vaynerchuk's WineLibrary.com personally calls every first-time customer just to say thank you. They don't turn the corner and try to upsell them. They just say, "Thank you for your business."

Delivering, consistently, is much easier said than done, so we've outlined a few simple steps to deliver on the promise.

Five steps to deliver on the promise

1. **Business plan** - Start small, focus on the right goals and write them down. Example: five new raving fans per month, not three percent conversion rates.

2. Marketing - Be real and show that you care; be visible and make sure it truly represents who you are. Example: "I'm a Mac; I'm a PC." Apple knew who they were and what they stood for when they ran those ads. We are not suggesting that your approach be this direct, but it may be the most specific example of this marketing tactic there is. This became highly memorable for Apple.

3. Communication - Respond immediately, casually and directly. Two thirds of people choose the first business that responds to them. Remember that conversions decay over time.

4. Interaction - Remove the friction and be available when you are needed. Example: if you sell real estate, you shouldn't be spending time on paperwork, you should be using systems like dotloop to remove friction so that you can focus on Peoplework.

5. Wow Factor - After the deal is done, do something amazing. Example: Random gifts, acts of kindness, things unimaginable to someone who invested in your product or services. Starbucks remembers your name, even though, at a company of that scale, it is difficult. At dotloop, we strive to be incredibly human and show that we care.

If you do this right, you will not have to ask for referrals. However, it will require focus and it will take time.

In the end, it is still a numbers game, but it turns out that this time less is more. Peoplework businesses spend less time and money on quantity (i.e., leads, advertising, etc.) and focus on quality. Know who you want to be, define your experience with the end user in mind and deliver on your promise every time. The rest will take care of itself, thanks to the newly established "people grid!"

Principle 6

SERVICE IS MARKETING

NOTHING INFLUENCES PEOPLE MORE THAN A
RECOMMENDATION FROM A TRUSTED FRIEND.

-MARK ZUCKERBERG

Historically, businesses have been taught to think about customer service as unavoidable overhead. For a Peoplework company, however, customer service is more than an overhead cost; it is marketing. Before the Peoplework era, we would invest in things like sales and marketing for growth, but the tables have officially turned. You can no longer separate service and marketing. Great service is great marketing and terrible service is terrible marketing.

Amazing service is delivered through a combination of people and products. In order to achieve great service, you have to set the vision and define a measurable experience. We touched on this in the previous chapter when we mentioned the customer experience that begins upon walking into a Starbucks. There are three basic rules to providing amazing service: provide options, deliver value and utilize marketing tools.

Service is a big part of the customer's overall experience, and, for a company to truly master service, they must visualize the experience from the customer's point of view. When you run a quality-first company and obsess over service, customers will come back for more and bring their friends with them.

Whether you are in the goods or services business, in the Peoplework era, everything begins with the service you provide either through people or through the product. The product could be an actual product (like Square), or the product could be a service (like my wife Angela's condo decorating business). As we discussed in the chapter on People to People, choice is not an option in the pre-Peoplework era. The only thing that will set you apart is your product and your people, plus the service you deliver.

Consider this: do you want people to say good things about your brand, nothing about your brand, or bad things about your brand? Note that when a customer says nothing about your brand it is not a win because this does not generate new customers.

Now, understand that marketing does have a place, but you'll probably find more marketing value out of great service. So when you invest in marketing, that investment should provide some sort of valuable service.

Service is all about setting the right expectations and fulfilling them for the customer. The first step to achieving this is by viewing service as a way to grow your top line, and not as an unavoidable expense. When you see a customer through the lens of LTV, justifying the investment in service becomes easy. After you define what quality service means, you can benchmark against those expectations. Be available by giving the consumer options to connect with you or get the information they need. Deliver value, but do not expect anything in return.

Here Is How You Get There

The first step is to identify and understand the people channels for service at your company. In Angela's case, with her decorative painting business, she is in the services industry, so it has a lot to do with the way she interacts with her customers. Free estimates and friendly, non-salesy responses to online inquiries are some of her best service-as-marketing assets. In a call center, it could be the support representative's tone or their overall competency in making decisions and creating solutions. It could come down to something like hold times or call times. Then think about a company like Square, which is more of a product business. In Square's case, the people side might include how they would handle fraud. Or it may have more to do with the device itself. Is it easy to obtain and use? How much value does it provide? Does it service the customer in ways that causes them to talk about it? If you're in the software business, it's about transitioning from a "software as a service" mindset to a "service as a service" mindset. The service is the software and everything that comes with it, from fulfillment, to support, and so on.

Once you understand your service channels, you're ready to define your vision.

Building on the last chapter's message about visualizing the experience from the customer's perspective, your vision for the service should have everything to do with delivering the best experience for your customers. To get there, you have to visualize "best experience" from the customer's perspective, and then benchmark against their expectations. When someone reaches out to a call center, if they get an answer in less than two minutes, the expectations are exceeded. If you are a premium/elite member, however, you likely expect a higher level of service. For example, Chris' Delta rep picks up in less than ten seconds because he is a Diamond member. This is service that exceeds his expectations and keeps him a satisfied customer. If his response time were less, it would affect his future expectations of the company.

YOU HAVE TO VISUALIZE "BEST EXPERIENCE" FROM THE CUSTOMER'S PERSPECTIVE

The good news is that, if someone knows they are getting a premium level of service, they recognize that and rave about it. Mostly, this is the case because the service is amazing, but also because people like to talk about what they have. The secret to pulling off this vision at scale is to have a clear understanding of your customer profiles and then define service levels for each. The goal is that the service level of your lowest tier still be higher than that of your competitor's highest. Your customer profiles might look something like this: User A is a monthly user with three-minute hold times (still above normal), User B with thirty-second hold times (way above normal), and so on.

Whether your business requires a "Delta Diamond" line or not, the fact of the matter is that, in a Peoplework economy, service is a priority because it brings referrals and referrals bring growth. So don't skimp on your vision!

Once you define your company's vision and expectations, there are three rules that must be followed:

1. Be Available By Giving The Consumer Options

These options include not only online information, but also phone/chat availability. Most technology companies drive all users to an online wiki or knowledge base. They do this mostly for financial reasons, particularly when the product is free, but even paid services sometimes do not offer phone support. Peoplework businesses give the customers options in the ways they can connect.

The Butterball Company gave their customers a great option on Thanksgiving Day by using Google Helpouts. They offered free live chat, called their "Turkey Talk-Line," which provided expert tips and advice to help cooks prepare their holiday meal at home. [xxi] What a valuable resource!

Now, in no way does this mean you cannot charge for those options, but they should still be available. For example, Evernote monetizes their premium services by having customers pay for Live Chat. That is how valuable talking to a human has become. Curaytor (Chris' company) is an entire business built around monetizing service, not software. As Chris puts it, "Software at Curaytor (and at dotloop) is simply an enabler of the service we focus first and foremost on." If a user would prefer to jump on a call or have their assistant jump on a call, as opposed to sorting through the knowledge base, they should have that option, even if they have to pay for it.

The inverse is also true. You cannot just provide the phone number and not an online knowledge base. Some people do not want to talk to another person, and the better the knowledge base gets, the more people will trend in that direction.

2. Deliver Value And Don't Expect Anything In Return

If your customer asks you a question (inbound activity), you should always answer it without trying to sell them something. Angela answers questions on Houzz; Gary V. answers wine questions on Twitter; Chris is active in Facebook Groups.

Answers to customer questions should to be functional, relevant, and appropriate. Also, do not underestimate the importance of timeliness. Getting a fast response is unbelievably valuable to your clients. The same is true of outbound activities. If you are going to host a webinar, do not do it to only sell your product, do it to deliver content that is valuable to the attendees even if they do not buy. This is what providing a service entails. If you do this right, you will end up making more sales without "selling" at all. Just remember that when you deliver value without expecting anything in return, you'll end up with more than you would have had you focused on the "ask" before the "give."

3. Provide Better Than Useful Service...for Free

There is a lot to be learned from the freemium business model, which gives away a product or service without asking customers for anything in return, but predicts that a portion of those free users will find enough value in the service that they're willing to pay for more of it. This strategy delivers a lot of value to a large base of users for free, and creates quality-paying users with little to no additional marketing involved. Companies like Evernote, MailChimp and Dropbox are a few perfect examples. If customers believe that a more desirable service exists beyond what is free, eventually a percentage of those users will decide to purchase the upgrade. Jeff Bezos once said that he does not want to make a profit on the Kindle, so it is sold at prices that break even. The low price expands their customer pool and ensures that people will continue to buy content from them through the hardware. This delivers more value and profits over time.

We've pursued a similar strategy at dotloop. Of the millions of people on our network, only a couple hundred thousand are paid users. It's a long-term strategy, but ultimately if you're providing a service that people value, people will be willing to pay for it. Delivering great service will bring great reward.

If you believe that amazing service is enough to keep people coming back and to get them to tell others about it, that is all you need to know. Put your eggs in that basket because investing in service will produce better results as a sales and marketing tool over time. This doesn't mean that you shouldn't continue to invest in sales and marketing, you should. But when Peoplework businesses invest in marketing, they purposefully do it in a way that provides a service. (See examples in Case Studies below.)

So visualize your plan, deliver value expecting nothing in return, and provide a service that is better than merely useful. Following this model, you will not have to ask for anything in return.

CASE STUDIES

SERVICE IS MARKETING IN ACTION

Square

Square, Inc. is an app for merchant services and customers that allows purchases to be made directly from a mobile device. Square was founded in 2009 by Jack Dorsey and Jim McKelvey as a way to provide a service to businesses and customers that helped them accept payments and purchase items using stored credit card information. The app works by manually entering the credit or debit card information or swiping it with the Square Reader, a device that is plugged directly into the smartphone or mobile device that reads the magnetic strip on the card. Once you are logged into the app, the interface is set up to look just like a traditional cash register for you to type in the credit card information.

Jack Dorsey first got the idea for Square when his friend, Jim McKelvey, couldn't complete a sale because his business did not accept credit cards. From this, a great idea was born. Dorsey and McKelvey wanted to provide a service to merchants and customers that helped them make any purchase or sell without hindrances. Square is free to download from the App Store or Google Play Store.

For every transaction that passes through the Square Reader, the company charges a 2.75% fee, and a monthly fee of $275 for those with yearly credit card transactions totaling less than $250,000. Even though this fee is higher than some of its competitors, Square proudly claims that its costs are the lowest because it has no hidden fees like other credit card companies. The top users of Square's app are food truck operators and consultants.

Square has been praised for its simple and sleek design, and its ease of use. Its goal is to provide a better product and service for its customers in order to help entrepreneurs grow their businesses. Square has received lots of recognition that has helped to grow the business. In 2012, Starbucks announced that it would use the Square Reader for any customers paying with a debit or credit card. [xxii]

Mophie

Based in California, Mophie is a designer and manufacturer of mobile intelligent devices and accessories. Mophie has won awards and been widely recognized for its creative designs and innovative solutions. If you've ever heard of the Juice Pack, the very first portable battery case certified by Apple Inc., then you have come face-to-face with a Mophie product. Their products are known to be seamless integrations of industrial, electronic, artistic and software designs. Mophie products can be found just about everywhere in retail, including Apple Stores, Best Buy and AT&T stores. Mophie products are not only useful, but also necessary.

The experience is so positive that, from the second you start using a Mophie product, you tell all of your friends, or they ask you what it is! The marketing that Mophie does is simply providing a service that is needed in a simple, beautiful and affordable way. "The first company — whether it's an incumbent phone maker or Ph.D.-laden start-up in a garage — that figures out how to solve the smartphone battery problem will see enormous gains," Farhad Manjoo wrote on TechCrunch.

Mophie was founded by Ben Kaufman when he was just 18 years old and currently clears about $5 million in annual revenue. [xxiii]

TripIt

"There's an app for that" has become a phrase that everyone is used to hearing, and the field of travel planning is certainly in the loop. When planning a trip, especially if you are a frequent traveler, it can be hectic and chaotic, but the goal of TripIt is to bring calm to the chaos and peace of mind to the traveler. TripIt was created in October 2006 as a free app. Once customers use the app, they then have access to all of its services. These services include organizing all travel plans like booking airline tickets, travel expenses, hotel confirmations and travel itinerary for when you reach your destination. With all that TripIt provides, it's surprising that it's free. However, TripIt focuses on the service it provides to its customers as a way to market the product. To its free users, TripIt offers premium features, like instant alerts for flight changes and better seating options, which can help to ease the stress of traveling.

The company has recently launched an extension of its original app by introducing TripIt for Teams. This is one of its premium services offered to groups or organizations to help with their travel planning. These services can be used on the iPhone, iPad and iPod Touch and come with a monthly payment. TripIt for Teams has everything that the original TripIt has with added bonuses like being able to track your travel destinations from your mobile devices and alerts for other team members who are traveling to the same destination. TripIt encourages social media sharing inside of the app, which provides powerful word-of-mouth marketing. TripIt has recently been acquired by the travel management company Concur. [xxiv]

Charmin

Back in 2006, the toilet tissue company, Charmin, decided to capitalize on the thousands of New Yorkers passing through the city during the holiday season and create a service to them at no cost.

A free 20-stall public restroom was built in Times Square, the heart of New York City, packed with Charmin toilet tissue and armed with attendants to keep it clean. For those waiting to use the restroom, Charmin provided a seating lounge and photo opportunity with the stuffed Charmin bear. Charmin advertised the event, and even invited celebrities to join in.

This was an ingenious idea from Charmin. By providing this free service to New Yorkers, they were also able to market their company and product. In order to do this, they did have to spend some money on marketing up front. Research says that Charmin spent approximately $150 to $225 a square foot per year, for the 7,000- to 8,000-square-foot space.

Follow-up research showed that there was a definite increase in Charmin's sales, and that even three months later, people remembered the Potty Palooza, as Charmin calls its spiffed-up johns. It turned out that it was money well spent for the large revenue that Charmin expected to receive from the word-of-mouth advertising about its product from every person using their restrooms. [xxv]

Principle 7

BUSINESSES ARE BUILT
ON COMMUNITIES

" NEVER DOUBT THAT A SMALL GROUP OF THOUGHTFUL CITIZENS CAN CHANGE THE WORLD. INDEED, IT IS THE ONLY THING THAT EVER HAS.

-MARGARET MEAD

Customers used to be acquired through access and distribution; that is, until the digital grid made access and distribution ubiquitous. Now the world is connected thanks to digital innovation. In many ways, this makes it easier to gain access to a world of potential customers. However, this blessing is also a curse. With our heads so buried in our iPhones, the digital grid has a tendency to disconnect us during people-to-people transactions, if we don't take the time to truly connect. At least that's the risk. Additionally, the abundance of connectedness, made available via the digital grid, also introduced a great deal of chaos, making it difficult to sort through the noise.

In the Peoplework era, the most successful businesses overcome the noise and stay connected by building communities. Communities are real and scalable, while maintaining a level of people-to-people intimacy. Communities grow organically and cut through the noise because people want to be with people they trust and with whom they share a common ground or belief system.

In order to better understand communities, let's examine the age-old customs of tribes. Entrepreneur, bestselling author and blogger Seth Godin has coined the popular word "tribe" in defining any group of people, large or small, who are connected to one another, a leader and an idea. In his bestselling book of the same name, Godin states that individuals are all leaders, leading others at varying levels within our organizations and our communities. This is how tribes are built.

It's worth noting that tribes are not built accidentally. They require a purpose-driven leader and alignment around tribal values within the organization or community. And this requires a strong connection, which is where the community comes in. Connecting with an individual is not enough, we need the community grid; communities are an absolute necessity. [xxvi]

The Benefits of Community

Kickstarter may be the premier example of leveraging a tribe. For the book you are reading right now, we used this crowdfunding platform and successfully raised $73,000, making us one of the most funded books on Kickstarter of all time. Remember, we are first-time authors, not Seth Godin (who raised $228,000 in his first attempt at Kickstarter!). Here is why we had success. Let's say we went about the Peoplework Kickstarter campaign by saying, "Hey guys, we are selling this new book and we would like for you to buy it." How do you think that would go over versus: "Hey community, we are passionate about putting people first (something that our community can connect with and get behind). We are so passionate about it that we spent the last six months writing a book about it. That book is called Peoplework. We would love your help, as our community, to share this message with the world."?

As you might imagine, we took the latter approach and the results now speak for themselves. Through Kickstarter, we received the funding we needed, not because people were buying a book, but because they were supporting a common purpose that was shared by the community. During the process, we were hyper-sensitive to the fact that maybe not everyone wanted to or could spend thirty dollars on a book. So, through Kickstarter, we allowed people to buy one chapter for three dollars. The irony is that, in large part, they did not choose the three-dollar option. Instead, they made an average contribution of two hundred and eighty-one dollars! We never expected this outcome. It's a testament to the power of community.

THE KEY TO BUILDING A COMMUNITY IS THAT THEY ARE INVOLVED ON DAY ONE, AND BEYOND

The key to building a community is that they are involved on day one, and beyond. After the Kickstarter campaign wrapped up, we kept the community updated using Kickstarter's messaging feature. We shared with the early supporters of the book things like a first look at book's website, a first look at the book's cover and even let them read the entire Intro as well as Chapter one first. We held free webinars where we dissected one Peoplework principle at a time, even making changes to the book based on questions from the community during the calls. I wrote articles about Peoplework for Inc. that didn't sell the book; they sold the purpose of putting people first in a digital-first world. My co-author Chris continued to keep the community in the loop using his popular weekly live Google+ Hangout, #WaterCooler. He even auctioned off his personal business book collection, using eBay, as a way to buy free books for the community at large (special thanks to John Mangas, who spent $355 to buy the collection).

The truth is that the tribe of people that originally rallied behind Peoplework was not very large. Several hundred people at the most. But their passion (and sense of ownership) is what led this book to having a first print run of more than 10,000 copies. Even the future of books is going to be controlled by people, not publishers!

Now, apply this same example to your community. Whether you sell real estate, automobiles or software, it's about assembling a group of people whose faces you frequently see, whom you sometimes interact with and whom you trust. And they trust you as well. All of these things together, along with shared passion, build communities.

You used to join communities because you had to. If you wanted to buy something at a discount you bought at Walmart. Now? Websites like Groupon, Fab, Woot and countless others have commoditized access and distribution. Now Walmart is just one of many options to get low prices.

Translate this to the business world. Most businesses have a database, and they communicate with that database as a group of people to whom they want to sell products. If your goal is to increase sales, imagine the power of offering something special to your community because you care about them. Or, if your goal is to announce a new product, imagine if you polled your community for their feedback and then thanked them for their input once the product was available. The concept is very simple: people want to be part of something that matters, especially when they're doing it with like-minded people they trust. A Peoplework company understands the importance of leveraging their community in order to build their brand. When multiple people align around a common purpose, a sense of community evolves.

Four Tribal Rules to Follow

Tribal leaders and companies embody a few characteristics that result in passionate followings. They do not exist to sell a product. They exist for a greater purpose and they are clear about that purpose in everything they do, from the way they manage, to the values, to the priorities, to the communication styles, etc. They do less talking and more facilitating. Their long-term point of view acknowledges that people build communities and that their job is to cultivate and facilitate forums in which those communities can communicate and grow. Building communities is like investing for retirement — it takes a long time to build, but once it grows, it compounds and someday it becomes a large amount of money.

1. Exist for a greater purpose, not to sell products

Tribal businesses exist to solve a bigger problem. 37signals, for example, exists to make project management collaborative and frustration-free. Apple exists to think differently and challenge the status quo. Evernote has set out to help the world capture memories. dotloop exists to help people work better together. Communities at this scale were not possible before the mid-2000s, which was pre- social, pre-mobile and pre-Peoplework. Communities are built around passion and purpose, not features and functions.

2. Content Marketing Builds Tribes

When referring to companies like Dell, IBM, Blockbuster, Kodak or Borders, the question becomes: What could their communities have been? (Oops, many of them are not even here anymore. Had they leveraged their community, their business model would have evolved better/faster.)

Netflix (the modern-day Blockbuster) is now investing in original programming (like House of Cards and Orange is the New Black). Those shows are building the Netflix community much more than purchasing a season of Breaking Bad would. What if Netflix went even further and built (or acquired) a mobile app like Get Glue? It's a socially infused platform for watching TV, Movies and Sports with your friends. Imagine the larger connection and community that could be built.

On AMC's The Walking Dead, the community is so passionate about the show that AMC recognized that and created another hour- long show, which airs directly afterwards, called The Talking Dead. The entire purpose of The Talking Dead is for the community to gather and talk about the show they literally just finished watching! They field real-time questions from Facebook, Twitter and the studio audience and bring on the community's favorite characters and even the show's writers and producers. Access equals community.

In each of these situations, the followings that formed around the business happened because they believed in the purpose and felt a sense of ownership in the vision. The content under the hood was worth following. Take 37signals, for example. They are a "privately held American web application company" focusing on providing the best web-based experience for their community of clients. The vision of 37signals is to provide simple, feature-lite products that make project management frustration-free, in order to be effective for those in their community. The people who invest in their software are completely okay with that. [xxvii]

Gary Keller and Keller Williams Realty have formed the largest residential real estate company in North America, not by selling real estate, but by building a sense of community and ownership in something meaningful, a family. For Keller Williams, family is about helping people, growing communities, and building financial security for yourself and the people you care about. It is a business built around people, and it has become highly contagious. On the flip side, other brands created their own community. RE/MAX for example, created a very different, but equally impressive, type of community around them first in order to drive the brand. When you go to a Keller Williams event, it's about culture and family. When you go to a RE/MAX event, it's all business and brand. Neither approach is right or wrong; the thing to take away is that each company is incredibly successful in its own way and each has a strong community that makes it possible.

In all of the examples mentioned above, these things did not happen organically. They happened over time and because effective leaders and companies formed genuine connections, purposefully. Remember that change requires a blueprint, so carve out time for community. Change and passion are the new sales and marketing.

3. Stop Selling Immediately

The traditional business exists to sell products. However, this mindset is not sustainable or meaningful, and people can't get behind it. Defining the greater purpose, however, is just the first step. Tribal leaders need to make the purpose a core part of who the company is by making it highly visible in the company values and communication, and reinforce it both externally and internally. When you exist for the greater purpose and not to sell products, you won't have to sell. At dotloop, we like to say it's about Peoplework, not paperwork. In the end, it's about benefiting the community of people. So we only do things that tie back to the purpose of helping people work better together. I mention this because "not selling" can be difficult at times. For example, if a big customer says: "We will buy, but only if you add X, Y, Z features to the system," the temptation is to add those features to get the deal, but that doesn't scale and it's not consistent with our vision. We exist to help people work better together and we build products to support that purpose. We won't allow ourselves to become distracted just to make a sale.

4. Less Talking and More Facilitating

Communities are powerful, but they need to have a place for individuals to talk and grow. This can be difficult for companies because you have to be able to tolerate hearing the good, the bad and the ugly. You must have thick skin and have an appreciation for transparency, and you must create forums for people to communicate.

Start with Surveys, aka Listening

Listening to your customers is key. The surveys should start with: "Our goal is to [INSERT PURPOSE]. Tell us how we are doing and what else we could do to enable that purpose for you." Trust me, people want to be heard. If you don't know where to start, Survey Monkey is a great software option to facilitate online surveys. The CEO of Second Life even emails his entire staff quarterly to simply ask if he should still be CEO!

Facebook Group forums provide another great community builder platform. It wasn't always easy for people to find one another. Thanks to the digital revolution, it is very easy for a company to make that possible now. As an example, we have open forums in real estate. Within those groups, the community socializes about anything they wish. Two Facebook Groups Chris runs, which have seen the most success, are Tech Support Group for Real Estate Agents and What Should I Spend My Money On? At dotloop, we have several active forums for different segments of our community. They are both focused entirely on the community helping the community. People-to-people. That being said, the Groups have a leader. The leader benefits from the Groups as much as the Groups benefit from the leader. As Rudyard Kipling so eloquently put it, "The strength of the wolf is the pack and the strength of the pack is the wolf."

Many companies also use a forum such as a blog to discuss a purpose and to feature others that blog on the same common purpose. What tends to happen is that others who share in that purpose follow the blog and engage regularly. Copyblogger.com, SocialTriggers.com, TwistImage.com/blog and ChrisBrogan.com are amazing examples of this. What they all figured out is that what you do on the other three hundred and sixty-four days a year that you are not selling is what matters most on the day you do.

At dotloop, whenever possible, we strive not to talk about what we do for our customers, but what our customers are doing in their own businesses to work better together. This may seem counterintuitive, but guess what, dotloop is a part of that, which resonates with their community. By helping our customers, we are in essence helping ourselves. That is the essence of Peoplework: when people help each other, everyone wins. It's a different way to communicate. Instead of talking about yourself, it is about others talking about the greater purpose.

As your community talks, you can contribute, but you have to contribute as a member of the community, not as an employee trying to sell a product. It has to be a natural evolution and an organic movement that evolves with time. Building communities is like investing.

Words Matter, A Lot

One thing that you will see within most great communities is that people speak a common language. At Starbucks you do not order a large, instead it is a Venti. Keller Williams does not have a Broker, instead they have Team Leaders. At dotloop we do not use the terms contracts or deals, instead we call them loops. People's sense of community increases when they feel like a part of something special. Those are the types of things that great companies will cultivate within a community — a sense of solidarity.

And then, once your community talks, you need to listen and act on a regular basis.

YOU NEED TO LISTEN AND ACT ON A REGULAR BASIS

In a product forum, as an example, you should not be defensive, but instead be contributing, listening and actively engaging as a member of the community. When you respond, let your community know that you have heard their feedback and what you are doing about it. Also, tell them that you welcome continued feedback. It's not about creating a language just for the sake of creating one. It's about making the community feel as if they are a part of something bigger than themselves. The customers, and your community members, need to feel as if they are a part of a different experience.

Thinking Long-Term

Building communities is not a get-rich-quick play. It takes time and patience, and the results are not always immediately obvious. Think of it like investing: if you invest one thousand dollars per month in a savings account that generates ten percent interest per year, the twelve thousand dollars in savings might not feel like a ton of money. But, that one thousand dollars per month will turn into millions over time.

Communities grow in a similar manner. Before Justin Bieber was Justin Bieber, there was a time when he only had forty Twitter followers (instead of 40 million). But even then, he still showed his appreciation for the community of 40. He understood the power of community. What you focus on, you will find. Similarly, Taylor Swift's staff hand-picks people randomly in each city as opposed to the traditional prearranged meet and greet. Her purpose connects to people. It's the small things, consistently, that become big over time.

WHAT YOU FOCUS ON, YOU WILL FIND

Business communities can scale just as quickly as a pop star's community. Just look at how Instagram, Pinterest and Facebook have grown. The challenge for most businesses and business leaders, however, is to think long-term. Why? Most businesses are generally measured over the short term. Investors and markets focus month-to-month or quarter-to-quarter. Communities do not pay dividends over a quarter. Think of it this way, if you focus only on your checking account instead of your savings, you will end up living check to check, not establishing the long-term benefits of saving.

A great example of a long-term thinker in business is Jeff Bezos of Amazon.com. Jeff is famous for thinking long-term, which was first marked by a 1997 shareholder letter that explained his long-term view and willingness to be misunderstood for a quite awhile. (See pplwork. com to find the 1997 shareholder letter.)

Or Mark Zuckerberg, who had lots of pressure to sell his business for billions of dollars and think about Facebook as only a "college thing." He refused to sell because he had a long-term purpose to connect the world, not just college campuses. It wasn't about dollars and cents, it was about a purpose and community. [xxviii]

It takes discipline to think long-term because you are at odds with ninety-nine percent of the business community. And as a leader with shareholders, investors, or people who depend on you, you will be at odds with ninety-nine percent of them as well. Community is a different way of thinking — a long-term play. Community is at conflict with the way that most businesses work, but a Peoplework company welcomes the challenge because they recognize the value in the long-term.

The most successful Peoplework businesses build communities around their purpose. People want to be part of something, but those communities do not form by accident. They will be formed by tribal leaders and businesses that value people, purpose and passion. To get there, you have to exist for a greater purpose and be a long-term thinker. Once you start the community, and continue to cultivate it, the power will grow in time and eventually stand on its own. Create a Create a community that is as vested as you are, and good things will follow!

COMMUNITIES DO NOT FORM BY ACCIDENT

CASE STUDIES

COMMUNITIES IN ACTION

dotloop

At dotloop, we leverage communities to not only engage with existing customers, but also to further our reach and influence within the real estate space. When we first took on this initiative, we hired a full-time community manager whose primary responsibility is to ensure that we maintain a consistent and open channel of communication through social media. His success is measured by user engagement metrics, total online reach, and maintaining the "image" of our brand.

Our Community Manager has implemented policies such as "no tweet left behind," meaning that when someone mentions dotloop or discusses our solution, we directly engage with that individual. This policy has proven to be extremely beneficial. By investing in resources that help us manage our social presence, and dedicating one person to this role, we maintain a consistent message on all platforms, as well as have an intimate relationship with our customers. The sentiment here is that, by being "human" in our social media approach, our followers/fans/users develop a stronger connection to dotloop as a company.

Internally, we have a culture that utilizes some of the same principles that we used to build our external community. Since dotloop's creation, we've strived to maintain a strong and vibrant culture, and, in order to do so, we created our "culture committee." The culture committee consists of four individuals who help share company "wins," employee highlights, and are responsible for any company special events such as Christmas parties, etc. Throughout the office you will find our core values written on the walls, literally. This allows us to constantly be reminded of our company values, and helps keep us accountable to those values. Lastly, our central communication point is in our Facebook group called "in the loop...", where we openly discuss personal and professional feats, birthdays, marriages, etc. It's all about keeping each individual in the company connected with others so that we can all work better, together.

Additionally, we try to highlight our loopers (users) through various initiatives via social media and blogging. Peoplework profiles are probably our most frequently used methods, which allow us to create stories and articles highlighting our top users or our major advocates. These profiles allow our biggest fans to position themselves as industry leaders, and further allow us to highlight our community of users. [xxix]

Curaytor

In January 2013, my co-author Chris Smith announced his first ever startup, Curaytor. Chris co-founded the company with Jimmy Mackin and Andrew Leafe. Curaytor is a full-service digital marketing agency that develops software and provides customer support for top-producing real estate agents and real estate teams.

For the five years leading up to the launch of Curaytor, Chris, Mackin and Leafe had their finger on the pulse of the real estate technology space by listening the most, and then by helping as often as they could without asking for anything back. They accomplished this largely by building passionate communities using Facebook Pages and Facebook Groups. In 2009, as the communities started to grow and bond over a common passion (loving technology AND real estate), many other "thought leaders" were still questioning the validity of the platform.

As Mackin puts it, "We knew that the smartest person in the room (Facebook) was not us. It was the room itself. No one is smarter than everyone. We recognized that before most on social media. What we learned over that five-year period is directly responsible for our early success at Curaytor."

The founders also engage their community by hosting a live YouTube web show called #WaterCooler. They actually used a poll on Facebook empowering the community to choose the name of the program (Group member Andrew Machado suggested the name Water Cooler), and even allowing the community to decide the time and day of the week that the show airs (Group member Dale Chumbley suggested the Wednesday at 9:05pm slot). This is what a community is all about. It is so blindingly obvious through the actions they take, not just the words they say and the platforms they happen to use, that they care about and truly appreciate their tribe.

While still in their first year of operating (and with only six employees), Curaytor has crossed seven figures in annual revenue. Rare, and quite a feat, for any startup. [xxx]

PASSION POWERS PROFITS

 INSTEAD OF WONDERING WHEN YOUR NEXT VACATION IS, MAYBE YOU SHOULD SET UP A LIFE YOU DON'T NEED TO ESCAPE FROM.

-SETH GODIN

The startup world in the last couple of decades has shown us a new way to run a business. The "new" idea is about building a business around passion. Companies the likes of Google have pioneered the idea, and have been an inspiration for many other startups around the country. But what is this passion thing really all about? If you ask the average Fortune 500 executive, they would probably tell you it's just another goofy thing that those technology guys do. In the Peoplework era, however, passion is much more than a unique selling proposition. It's real, measurable, and critical to building a successful Peoplework business.

Anything outside of the typical office space arrangement would drive most working business people crazy. The traditional norms tell us to be professional, be proper and focus on efficiency and numbers. For this reason, unfortunately, passion is a topic that usually hits the back burner for most corporations. Contrary to what it might seem on the surface, passion is actually the most powerful asset a company can leverage to generate profits. It is even more powerful than professionalism, efficiency and the "numbers."

Passion is about more than a fun place to work, with free food and slushies — although those perks don't hurt. Passion is about people spending time on things that make them happy. In the Peoplework era, passion will produce the most profit.

The reason that most businesses focus on things like efficiency, revenue and profits, over passion, is because at the end of the day that is how we kept score. But take a minute and think about what puts numbers on the board. It all starts and ends with people, right? And people who spend time on things they are passionate about do better work. It should go without saying that better work puts numbers on the board. Peoplework businesses get this, and instead of focusing on the numbers first, they focus on the people first, specifically, how we make our people more productive through passion. One of the Quicken Loans ISMs sums up focusing on passion, not revenue, perfectly: "Numbers and money follow, they do not lead." [xxxi]

Passion Brings The Highest Return

Passion is what determines how much blood, sweat, tears and heart someone puts into their work! Take business out of the equation for a moment and let's pretend that you are passionate about fitness. You would make time for it. When you are exercising, you would give it everything you can. When you are not exercising, you would constantly be looking for ways to be more fit. You do not stop with exercise though; you would spend just as much energy maintaining a good diet. As a result, you would feel good about yourself and live a fit life.

Let's contrast this with someone who is not passionate about fitness. Regardless of what you tell them to do, you will see the following patterns: They will look for any excuse not to exercise because it will feel too much like "work." They will not make time for it, and they probably won't maintain a disciplined diet. As a result, they will not maintain a fit life.

Makes sense right? So now let's take a look at the typical work environment. We have found that most people work to live. Under this premise, you would choose jobs based on how much they pay, the quality of the benefits, the proximity of the job to your home, retirement plan, etc. You would think about work as something that we do to pay our bills and to save money. Along the way, in the back of your mind you would be thinking about that "magical" day —retirement. Simply put, people who work to live just work so that one day they won't have to.

As Steve Jobs so eloquently put it, "That is a pretty limited life." Here is why: under this scenario your job ends up being "work." Work for the sake of work is not fun, which is why people who work to live find the most happiness in Friday afternoons or vacations so that they don't have to work. Given that half of our lives are spent working, why would you spend half of your life on something you do not enjoy?

Passionate people, however, live to work. Not because they love work, but because their "work" coincides with their passion. As an example, I have as much or more fun at work as I do on weekends or vacation. It's the same reason that I end up working on weekends and during vacation. Not because I have to, but because I truly love what I do and I'm fueled by the stimulation that the daily challenge gives my heart and mind. The bottom line is that when your job is something you are passionate about you'll enjoy it. Passionate people do not dread Mondays; passionate people do not wait for the weekend to get away from work. When passionate people are on vacation, they are still working, not because they have to but because they want to. The question you must ask yourself is this: Am I happy with my life and how I am spending my precious time along this journey? Answering this question will give you clarity, and once you have clarity on what it is you enjoy and want to pursue, this will drive your passion. You may face challenges when pursuing your passion, but the real test is how you react to them. Clarity prevents you from becoming overwhelmed, and allows you to maximize every area of your life in order to continue pursuing your passion. Peoplework is about living to follow your passion.

Financial Vs. Emotional Profit

You probably interpreted the title of this chapter as suggesting that passion generates financial profit. It does. But by "profit," we intended something much broader. After all, wealth comes in many forms and financial wealth is just one of them. The other form of wealth is emotional in nature, which passion also fuels. This is an important point because it's easy to get caught up in the potential financial gains first. This is the wrong approach. Financial wealth does not buy happiness or emotional stability. It does buy options, which in many ways enable you to spend more time on things that make you happy. However, the one true form of wealth that buys happiness is being emotionally content.

When you have a clear view of what you are passionate about the Return on Investment (ROI) is pretty straightforward. If you enjoy what you do, you will have more fun doing it. You will work longer, harder, and most importantly, the output of your work will be better. When you produce better work, you feel more fulfilled. You will also feel better about yourself because you're doing something that you believe in. Following passion really is a self-fulfilling prophecy.

When you are pursuing your passion in business, you will end up surrounding yourself with people who are also passionate. This is because when you're passionate about something, you won't tolerate having non-passionate people around you. So as a business owner, you must surround the company with passionate people. When you do, your people will be happier and you'll benefit by getting more out of your people, in terms of both quality and quantity. Company morale will also be higher because everyone will be enjoying what they do, giving you fewer people problems to deal with when everyone is aligned around a common goal. All of this collectively means that the company will do better work and produce greater profits. That in turn, again, comes back around in the form of you living a more financially and emotionally healthy life.

The ROI is huge when you start with passion, and trust that the results will follow. This is easy to do in a Peoplework organization filled with passionate people. So surround the company with passionate people, and if you truly invest in that passion over time, it will generate significant and measurable returns.

A Culture of Creativity Fuels Passion

Cultivating passion in a business requires effort. It starts by surrounding the company with the right people. Zappos, for example, pays new employees two thousand dollars to leave the company within their first thirty days. They want to make sure that everyone there is passionate, not just looking for money and numbers. Regardless of how you go about it, passion needs to be a core part of the onboarding process, and the second that you sense an employee is not passionate, or not there for the right reasons, your immediate response needs to be to ask them to move on to another opportunity.

Within the workplace there also needs to be a sense of comfort and commonality. People want to be creative and express their own ideas, while sharing a common ground with those they work with. That has to be an integral part of the culture. Peoplework businesses understand that passion is the nucleus of great companies and great cultures. They start by surrounding the company with passionate people who share in a common goal, and then they quickly get rid of the ones that do not share in that passion. They also value passion so much that they create an environment that supports it.

In a recent Fast Company article, Dan Kurzius, co-founder of MailChimp, was quoted as saying, "We provide an environment that allows for, and encourages, acting on spontaneous creativity." When employees feel safe sharing their new ideas — no matter how seemingly goofy — and have the freedom to pursue them, good things ultimately arise. "I plant the seed and water it and then stand back and watch it grow," Kurzius says. MailChimp's CEO Ben Chestnut even outlined five rules for a creative culture:

1. Avoid rules. Avoid order. Don't just embrace chaos, but create a little bit of it. Constant change, from the top down, keeps people nimble and flexible (and shows that you want constant change).

2. Give yourself and your team permission to be creative. Permission to try something new, permission to fail, permission to embarrass yourself and permission to have crazy ideas.

3. Hire weird people. Not just the tattooed and pierced in-strange-places kind, but people from outside your industry who would approach problems in different ways than you and your normal competitors.

4. Meetings are a necessary evil, but you can avoid the conference room and meet people in the halls, the water cooler, or their desks. Make meetings less about delegation and task management and more about cross-pollination of

ideas (especially the weird ideas). This is a lot harder than centralized, top-down meetings. But this is your job — deal with it.

5. Structure your company to be flexible. Creativity is often spontaneous, so the whole company needs to be able to pivot quickly and execute on them (see #1). [xxxii]

Remember that finding passionate people is just the first step. To maximize its effect, you need to create a culture that enables passion to thrive through creativity.

Work Life Balance Always Matters

You also need to create an environment that supports the lifestyle. If people are coming to work to do what they enjoy, you'd better make sure the environment is enjoyable and supports some of the other constraints that life introduces. For example, most passion- centric companies have flexible dress codes (or in some cases, none at all) because they want people to feel comfortable. Part of spending your time enjoying what you do is having the freedom in how you do it — the freedom to be yourself. Passionate people will spend more time at work.

Some companies provide their employees with free food. If they are going to work all the time, they need to eat. Google, LinkedIn and many other popular tech companies are well-known for this. Marissa Mayer also implemented this within days of taking on the new CEO job at Yahoo. Other companies give their employees the freedom to work from home like 37signals (unlike Yahoo). Other companies will provide daycare for parents. All of these are great incentives to work harder toward individual and company passions. No one approach is right or wrong, the point is that each of these companies is investing in passion by creating the best environment for their people.

Beyond talking the talk, companies must also walk the walk. You have to operate your company in a way that is consistent with your proclaimed passion. Here are some examples: Whole Foods only supports organic foods; Toms is all about giving, and the entire culture supports that passion; Airbnb's founder lived in Airbnb-leased housing for years; Zappos built a service business that just happens to sell shoes. The cultures of these great companies, although different from company to company, are aligned around their stated passion. Investing in passion is not just a tech company thing, it is a people thing.

INVESTING IN PASSION IS NOT JUST A TECH COMPANY THING, IT IS A PEOPLE THING

Honing In On Your Passion

Mark Zuckerberg is the poster child example of a leader that has honed in on his passion. In fact, he breaks all of the traditional norms as we knew them in the past. We all know him for replacing the traditional suit and tie with a hoodie and sandals, but what everyone does not know is that, two years after starting Facebook, Mark was offered 1 billion dollars for his company by Yahoo. His immediate response to this offer was, "I don't know what I could do with the money. I'd just start another social networking site. I kind of like the one I already have." That approach is clarity around passion and by following his passion, Mark has become a very wealthy person, both emotionally and financially. [xxxiii]

The secret to getting the most out of both life and business is figuring out what you are passionate about and spending as much time as possible on that. It is why Zuckerberg turned down the money. It's why serial entrepreneurs don't stop working. It's why I don't stop working during weekends or vacations. Peoplework businesses, big and small, make passion a core part of who they are. Without it, your potential will be stifled, your morale will be average, and you'll be missing a huge opportunity to make a meaningful impact on people's lives and on the world at large.

Being a Peoplework business is not solely about driving a business' profits or working with people, it's mostly about understanding the value of our lives, and making the best of it. Once you find your passion and enable your people to do the same, your business will prosper. Prosperity will come in the form of both financial wealth and happiness. And while it's nice that financial wealth buys options, as you invest in passion, remember that the truest measurement of prosperity is happiness.

*****

CASE STUDY

PASSION IN ACTION

Steve Jobs

Earlier in this chapter I said that nothing matters more than maximizing every area of your life in whatever way you need to. In essence, nothing should stop you from following your passion. Steve Jobs is a great example of someone who knew what he was passionate about and consistently pursued it, even unto death.

It is widely known that Steve Jobs was one of the greatest innovators of our time. Throughout his life, he lived according to this mantra: "If today were the last day of my life, would I want to do what I'm about to do today?" Remembering that he would not live forever was an important tool in helping him follow his passion. He believed that in life, "You need a lot of passion for what you're doing because it's so hard. Without passion, any rational person would give up. So if you're not having fun doing it, if you don't absolutely love it, then stop doing it."

Steve Jobs exuded passion for his work, which enabled him to continue doing it. In addition, he had a team of people around him who fueled this passion and enabled him to do what he did well. Beyond business, Steve Jobs also had a passion for life.

Knowing that his life was coming to an end while in the final stages of cancer, Steve Jobs wanted to ensure that after his death there would be a purpose to his life and the lives of others. He planned every facet of his memorial service, from the entertainment to the guests to the gifts. His last gift was a brown box for everyone who attended his memorial service. Inside each box was a copy of the Autobiography of a Yogi by Hindu guru Paramahansa Yogananda.

In the same way that Steve Jobs had come to his own self-realization by pursuing his passion in life and finding happiness in it, he wanted to give that gift to others. [xxxiv]

STARS ARE MADE IN HOLLYWOOD

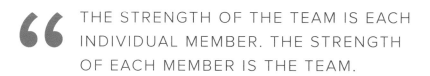

THE STRENGTH OF THE TEAM IS EACH INDIVIDUAL MEMBER. THE STRENGTH OF EACH MEMBER IS THE TEAM.

-PHIL JACKSON

Until now we have talked a lot about the fact that business is just about people doing business with other people. What is also true is that companies prosper and fail based on their people. So, it is time to look, both externally and internally, at whom you are surrounding yourself with. It is not a surprise that the best businesses have the best and most prominent people working for them, or that the greatest entrepreneurs are serial entrepreneurs. It is also not shocking that country singers come out of Nashville, or that most big tech companies come out of San Francisco. And it is not a surprise that most movie stars are made in Hollywood. This is not because the people in these cities are better than anyone else; it's simply a higher concentration of like-minded people.

These correlations are not coincidences. The people you surround yourself with are the people who influence who you will become and what you will achieve.

Now that the world is connected and digitized, the people who make up a business are more important than ever because they are the greatest differentiator. If you start with people in everything that you do, what you will find is that people are the most potent weapon that you have. If you ignore this principle, you'd be setting yourself up for failure. To summarize, if surrounding yourself with greatness was important in the industrial and digital revolutions, then it is the lifeblood of the Peoplework revolution.

Entrepreneurial Liberal Arts

Basic business principles about how economics, markets and finance work are critical skills for any entrepreneur. So, too, are critical thinking, communication, public speaking, leadership and group interaction skills. I studied architecture and real estate development as an undergraduate, but they didn't teach me Peoplework in school. So I experimented, read books, and, most importantly, I sought out successful people and learned everything I could from them. In fact, I believed in other people so much so that I pursued a law degree, not because I intend to practice law, but because a mentor whom I respected suggested that it would be an asset during my entrepreneurial journey. I respected his advice and knew that the same endeavor had paid massive dividends for him throughout his entrepreneurial journey. Understanding the need to grow yourself and master your craft, however, is just the beginning. The most successful entrepreneurs don't succeed alone. They need other successful entrepreneurs to learn from. Business is about people working with other people.

BUSINESS IS ABOUT PEOPLE WORKING WITH OTHER PEOPLE

Not everyone needs to be from Hollywood. I didn't come from Hollywood either. I attended a local public high school forty miles north of Cincinnati called Little Miami. It is a rural town and beautiful in many ways. The people are genuine, there's no such thing as traffic, and the abundance of land gives "peace and quiet" a new meaning. But what Little Miami is not is a hub for technology entrepreneurs.

To become a tech entrepreneur, I had to surround myself with people in that space. The first of many great people I surrounded myself with was my co-founder, Matt Vorst. I ended up moving into the city, Matt and I got involved in a number of the different entrepreneurial organizations, and we ultimately built an amazing business by surrounding the company with great and passionate people.

Whether you're from a rural town in southern Ohio or from Beverly Hills, if you want to make movies just know that your odds will be better in Hollywood.

Breaking Down The Ingredients

In business, the right environment makes a difference whether it is a small town, or a large city. You are an average of the five people you surround yourself with. So, if you are a real estate agent who wants to support a certain neighborhood, be present in that neighborhood. Be at all the events, walk the streets daily, eat at the restaurants and shop at the nearby malls. If you want to break into the country music industry, you'll have to make the sacrifice and move to Nashville, or at least spend some significant time there.

Let's glance into the technology world. It is no secret that big, world-changing Internet companies can be made anywhere. It happens all the time. dotloop is a prime example; we are proud to be from Cincinnati. But it's also no secret that the highest concentration of tech companies comes from San Francisco. Companies like Google, Twitter, Facebook and Apple, to name a few, are all based there. So what is it about San Francisco? It has a higher concentration and larger base of the right people for Internet businesses. Just look at the quantity of venture capital firms or the sheer dollars invested in San Francisco compared to other areas. It's not that other cities don't have the right people — they do, it is just that San Francisco has a higher concentration, which makes your odds better. So, at dotloop, we've decided to straddle both worlds by leveraging the best of what Cincinnati and San Francisco have to offer. You are a function of those around you.

People are just an average of those they hang around, which means that you need to be selective about who you surround yourself with. The evolution towards Hollywood, as we know it today, is a prime example of that. It did not become Hollywood overnight.

Hollywood, and the movie industry, has become synonymous with feelings of hope, fear, romance and dazzle. Yet, this wasn't always the case. The early 1890s marked the creation of the first motion picture camera by the employees of Thomas Edison's laboratories in New Jersey. [xxxv] For the first 15 years, New York/New Jersey dominated the movie industry, and Hollywood was only a small city somewhere in southern California.

Debates arise as to who was the first person to give Hollywood its name. Some accounts say that it was H. J. Whitley, known as the "Father of Hollywood," who was the first to name it.

In the early 1900s, movie making and the film medium were still very new and many Jewish immigrants found employment in the industry. Men like Samuel Goldwyn, Carl Laemmle, Adolph Zukor, Louis B. Mayer, and the Warner Brothers (Harry, Albert, Samuel, and Jack) are the famous names we now know to represent Hollywood. They moved to the production side of the business and became the leaders of the Hollywood movie studio.

Other moviemakers from Europe arrived in Hollywood after World War I, and soon hundreds of movies per year, seen by audiences of up to 90 million Americans per week, were being produced. Hollywood became the place where everyone wanted to be if they wanted to be in front or behind the movie camera.

Stars Are Made

Motion picture companies made lots of money as the movie making business experienced exponential growth. Thousands of people were given a salary: actors, producers, directors, writers, stuntmen, craftspersons, and technicians. Many great works of cinema came from this time period of filmmaking, including classics like: Casablanca, It's a Wonderful Life, the original King Kong, and Snow White and the Seven Dwarfs. [xxxvi]

George Clooney is originally from my hometown of Cincinnati, and, while I am certain that he had a wonderful childhood and still loves his hometown, it was Hollywood that made him famous. In order to pursue his dream of acting, he had to put himself in the right place, surrounded by the right people, and Hollywood was this place. The culture in Hollywood is that everyone is aspiring to get into acting, and the culture helps to make that happen, but not overnight.

You are a function of those you spend time with, and if you want to be a "star" in your business you must surround yourself with "stars" in your business. Your environment and the people you surround yourself with may not completely determine but will strongly influence who you become.

IF YOU WANT TO BE A "STAR " IN YOUR BUSINESS YOU MUST SURROUND YOURSELF WITH "STARS"

This same concept not only applies from an environment to a person, but inversely from people to an environment. Meet Over-the-Rhine. During a time of extensive German immigration in the nineteenth century and into the twentieth century, Over-the-Rhine, in Cincinnati, became a city that was notorious for its poverty. Reason Magazine labeled it as the "ground zero in inner-city decline," in 2001. In the 1970s there were many advocates who fought to preserve the city's history without simultaneously displacing its poor population. The 2001 Cincinnati riots put Over-the-Rhine on the map in a bad way and garnered lots of negative attention. This, in turn, hastened the population decline that had been going on for a century.

Property values declined and it presented an opportunity for developers to purchase, and subsequently renovate, a large number of historic buildings in the city. Many millions of dollars were spent to revitalize the city's neighborhoods. Since then, the crime rate has decreased each year, starting in 2006. The Cincinnati Enquirer described it: "in just six years, developers have moved Over-the-Rhine from one of America's poorest, most run-down neighborhoods to among its most promising," and according to the Urban Land Institute Over-the-Rhine is "the best development in the country right now."

Between 2001 and 2006, Over-the-Rhine had the highest number of violent crimes and robberies, the majority of them were drug-related. However, after 2005 the crime rate began rapidly decreasing. Law enforcement credits the city's redevelopment and population growth for this decrease. The neighborhood felt safer and attracted new businesses. According to reports, "A business owner reported that panhandling and shoplifting in his store dropped 90 percent after he moved from the Central Business District to Over-the-Rhine."

As of September 22, 2012, violent crimes and property crimes in Over-the-Rhine had "dropped 24% and 17% respectively," when compared to previous years. [xxxvii]

Over-the-Rhine is a great example that if you change the mix of people who inhabit a neighborhood, it changes the neighborhood.

And this can be applied to any city, any business, any market or target customer. Not only can an environment influence what people become, but people can also influence what an environment becomes.

Translating This To Business

Before the digital revolution, the way we choose the people we surrounded ourselves with was different than it is now. The composition of the people has changed. Building the right customer base is important to building the right company, and it is all about who you surround yourself and your company with. It does not mean you have to be in San Francisco as a tech company or in Hollywood as an actor, but your odds of success are much better if you are connected to the right people in those places.

YOUR ODDS OF SUCCESS ARE MUCH BETTER IF YOU ARE CONNECTED TO THE RIGHT PEOPLE

If you desire to be a successful Realtor specializing in high-end condos within a certain market, then you should probably live in a high-end condo in that market. You should hang out in the places where those residents frequent. Then, you will need to market to those living in high-end condos as well, with things that are relevant to them. It comes down to these three key points:

1. Living Proof - Surrounding the company with people who have been there and done that. Think about careers as a game of leapfrog. You jump along the way and you want the right people at the right times. Oftentimes in startups, people do not grow as fast as the startup, so make sure you put the right people in place with the right experiences at the right times.

The same is true for larger and more established businesses. If you need a turnaround, get a turnaround guy. If you want to build a retail store experience, get a retail guy. You cannot afford to have key people learn on the job.

2. Access to the network - It is true that it is all about who you know, not just what you know. If you are in show biz, you better have a connection to Hollywood. If you are in Consumer Packaged Goods, it would not hurt to be connected to Cincinnati. If you sell into Coca-Cola, it might not hurt to be plugged into Atlanta. Also, surround the company with the right people. Noel Fenton is the head of Trinity Ventures. We chose Noel and his firm as our Venture partner at dotloop because he was the right guy, with the right experiences, to help us get where we wanted to go. It was about Noel, and not the money. His access and experiences won. Cheaper money was available but the safest way to bet is on the best people.

3. Culture - Build a culture that supports what you are trying to become and get rid of people quickly who are bad for the culture; one bad egg spoils the dozen. Ideally, it all starts with putting the right people in the right places as the first solution. Noel always says my only two jobs as CEO of dotloop are getting the strategy right and putting the right people in the right places. But keeping the right people happy can be harder. You have to appreciate them. Did you know more people get divorced due to a lack of appreciation by their spouse than for any other reason? You have to appreciate your people. Empower them to pursue their dreams and the company dream. Position and help them be the best that they can be. Know that people require lots of work, so block lots of time for it. Acting fast enough on the bad eggs can be the hardest of all. Trust your gut and dig deep. Once you know it, you know it even if you do not have the data to support it, and the same goes for being in the right places. Some people can get you from A to B, but not C. Change will be constant. This is true in every business, but especially with startups and companies that experience above-average levels of growth and change.

We've talked a lot about putting the right people in the right places, and a little about acting on the wrong people in the wrong places. I just want to reinforce how important acting on the wrong people is. Because we are human and humans make mistakes. You will make people mistakes. When this happens, it's nearly impossible to act too fast. If your gut tells you someone is not right, and certainly if performance indicates the same, it is time to act. No one ever says "I fired too quickly," they all say "I waited too long." What's ironic about this statement is that it feels non-human on the surface. It's actually just the opposite. Enabling the wrong person to stay in the wrong position is a bad thing for the individual and for the business. The right thing to do is to help people find their passions and put them in positions to succeed. If that's not happening, fix it fast.

What's Your Personal Trajectory?

Doug Collins coached Michael Jordan from 1986–1989, [xxxviii] but could not reach the level of success necessary to win a world championship. Enter Phil Jackson and the rest is history. Jack Welch, legendary CEO of GE, would cut the bottom ten percent of the employees every year. He knew they would always grow. By simply bringing in new blood, and removing the bottom performers, it raised the bar. Some would argue that this approach is a bit harsh, but others would argue that this churn is healthy for the business. I wouldn't go as far as saying that you must churn 10% annually, but I would challenge you to challenge yourself and your people to raise the bar every month. When you're constantly raising the bar, you'll probably end up churning five to ten percent of your staff annually, and there's nothing wrong with that.

In the Peoplework era, people are everything and the pace of change is rapid, so just focus on surrounding yourself with the best people at all times and good things will follow.

To be the best, you have to surround yourself with the best. It's that simple. We do it in when we choose our friends. We do it when we choose our spouse. Whether you are a one-man band or massive corporation, success will follow surrounding yourself with the right people.

*****

CASE STUDY

STARS IN ACTION

Phil Jackson

Phil Jackson is widely regarded as the greatest coach in the history of the NBA. Under his belt Jackson has two championships as a player, holds the record for the most combined championships, totaling 13, and he holds 11 NBA titles as coach. Not to mention he has the highest overall winning percentage of any other coach. These are great accolades.

Jackson credits Eastern philosophy, as well as Native American spiritual practices, for his leadership approach. People refer to him as the "Zen Master." When asked how he manages his players so effectively, he said, "[I] use a lot of persuasiveness. You have to establish your philosophy and a system that embodies your fundamental approach. You have to be able to read failures and successes quickly, to make adjustments to your team so that there is constant growth. Finally, you have to have a long-range plan or long-range ideas, so you understand what is a good victory and what's an OK victory, what's a good loss versus what's a devastating loss."

Jackson made sure he treated his players as individuals and not just players. When asked about Michael Jordan he once said, "Michael Jordan is the epitome of what I call the peaceful warrior. His ability to stay relaxed and focused in the midst of chaos is unsurpassed."

When asked about Michael Jordan's teammates and how Jackson treated them in comparison to a player like Jordan, Jackson stated that he tried to include other elite players like Scottie Pippen at the same level as Jordan. He didn't elevate Jordan above the other "stars."

In addition, in order to become stars, stars also need co-stars (Pippen), and directors (Jackson), who will walk beside them, support them and push them to get better.

There are also people in your company who are going to be role players, like what Dennis Rodman was for the Bulls. When asked specifically about Rodman, who many fans and reporters labeled "troubled," Jackson had this to say: "I think the other players see Dennis as a special, talented person who has come into this business without as many advantages as others...he didn't start the NBA until he was 25. He's risen to his stature in an ungainly way. So the players were accommodating to him."

Your team will inevitably have a Rodman or two. Your leadership will directly dictate how they will be treated, and hopefully best leveraged, at your company.

Jackson is an example of someone who is passionate about people working better together. This is what Peoplework is about. As Jackson puts it, "Basketball is a team game... You've got to have five guys working together like the fingers on the hand, and until that happens you're all going to stick out in an awkward way." ^{xxxix}

ONLY YOU WRITE YOUR STORY

Principle 10

THE DIFFERENCE IN WINNING AND LOSING
IS MOST OFTEN, NOT QUITTING.

-WALT DISNEY

When you are born, the world already seems to exist for you. Then, as you grow and learn, the rules you are taught to follow and the concepts that are presented as fact all shape your perception of the world and how it works. Specifically, most people in society think about the world as a place where the boundaries are defined, and things just are what they are. The truth is that you can change the world and write your own story, but you must think about the world differently.

There are many entrepreneurs out there right now writing their own story. Steve Jobs challenged, and subsequently changed, the way people look at and use computers. The founders of Square challenged the status quo and wrote their own story about how we use currency, creating a device that allows anyone to easily accept payments using their smartphone or tablet. Elon Musk, another inspiring entrepreneur who lives without seeing limits on what is possible, started: Tesla, SpaceX and Hyperloop. With Tesla, Musk believes we do not need gas, as we have known it, to power the automobile. In SpaceX, he founded a company with the ultimate goal of "enabling people to live on other planets." Musk most recently released his blueprint for the Hyperloop, a new kind of "train" that can cross the entire United States in less than four hours. Musk refuses to let cars, trains and space exploration exist the way they always have, and constantly seeks new ways to challenge the status quo. His companies will revolutionize the way we travel. [xl]

The industrialized world, as we know it, was designed by people just like you and me, so why should we have to live within set boundaries? That is a limited life. You can change the world.

YOU CAN CHANGE THE WORLD

Do not live as if you can't. What you focus you will find. It all starts by recognizing that only YOU write your story. Peoplework leaders recognize that the world is shaped by people like you and me refusing to live within the boundaries we are born into.

Believing that you can change the world means adjusting your perspective. What sets entrepreneurs like Musk and Jobs apart from everyone else is their way of thinking. But like Musk or Jobs, you can adjust the way you think as well, by seeing the world through the lens that anything can be changed.

Kaihan Krippendorff of Fast Company said it best when he stated that in order for anyone to come up with the innovative ideas of entrepreneurs like Musk, Jobs and others, "We must reframe our thinking and develop: Visionary thinking, Systems thinking, Creative thinking, Critical/analytical thinking and Influential thinking." [xli]

The Power, And Challenge, Of Saying No

In order for Steve Jobs to write his own story and create an amazing digital user experience blending art and science into an incredibly simple and elegant technological design, he had to create a closed environment. This closed environment meant that Jobs and Apple would only support things that did not compromise their vision.

The most notable example was their relentless opposition to Flash, a software platform used to display animated graphics, games and videos on the Internet. No one else, at the time, had rejected using Flash because it was the standard. The resistance from Apple meant that any website, application, or video that was built to be supported by Flash could not be viewed on an Apple mobile device. Of course, the news of this spread and there was much controversy. However, Apple never relented. Eventually, Steve Jobs did change the world with his products, including the way people thought about Flash and the user experience today. [xlii]

Believing requires conviction. Conviction not only enables you to say no where necessary, it allows you to resist what all other rational people would see as irresistible. Once you believe that you can change the world, there are a few things you should know to make it happen.

Big Hairy Audacious Goals (BHAG)

In life and business, you have to think big to go big. You have to believe that the impossible is possible. Think BHAG. You may be changing the world in a certain way for the first time, but there are always things to be learned from others who have come before you. They set BHAGs too. I have studied Steve Jobs and go back to him for context and inspiration regularly. It is also true that if you set a BHAG without instilling the accountability points, it is incredibly difficult to maintain discipline. There is really no point in setting a Big Hairy Audacious Goal unless you are going to do everything you can to hit it, and if you do not, hold yourself accountable to those results, then pivot accordingly to try again.

YOU HAVE TO BELIEVE THAT THE
IMPOSSIBLE IS POSSIBLE

I set the Big Hairy Audacious Goal of running a marathon in two hours and thirty minutes. (That works out to five minutes and forty-three seconds per mile, for twenty-six miles.) Said differently, that's about ten minutes away from the current Olympic qualifying time. When I set this goal, my personal best was two hours and fifty-two minutes (six minutes and thirty-three seconds per mile), and even that personal best was eight minutes faster than my typical time of around three hours. But, after watching the 2013 Cincinnati Flying Pig Marathon and seeing the first finisher come across the line, I was inspired to run another marathon after a four-year break. Watching that finisher cross the line in the sub 2:30 range inspired my BHAG. He proved that it was possible. Despite the fact that I was only a recreational runner, I wanted to perform like the elite. I wanted to run in the 2:30s, which at the time felt impossible.

So, I immediately told my wife, my friends and family, and I wrote it on my wall, that I was going after a two-hour and thirty-minute time.

I was not sure how I was going to get there since I could barely run three miles at a five-minute forty-three-second pace, much less twenty-six miles, but setting my BHAG did not require knowing how, just the belief that there was a way.

Believing is just the beginning, from there, you have to do everything you can to make that belief become a reality. I immediately hired a coach, wrote my goal on the wall and told the whole world about what I was doing. I also signed up for the marathon to make it real. Then, I started waking up at 4:30am every day to train before work, which I did for a grueling five-plus months despite extensive travel and a very busy work life. My coach put together my plan, taught me some basic disciplines around form and technique, and reinforced that this was possible by showing me what others before me had done to achieve the 2:30 goal.

One of the mental challenges with marathon running or any goal you are determined to accomplish is that, when you are trying something that has not been done before, it is easy to give up. Just imagine running at 4:30am EVERY day, rain or shine, injured or healthy. With any real challenge, there is no shortage of temptations to give up. This is why it's important to make your commitment real. I wrote my goals down everywhere because it reminded me multiple times per day about what I said I would do. I told everyone I could, not because I wanted them to know, but because I wanted myself to be accountable to someone. I knew that I would let them down if I did not achieve my goal, which in turn would let me down. I was fully committed.

Sacrifice Is Necessary

In order to prepare for the marathon, I changed my diet and daily schedule immediately. I went from running three to four miles a few times per week to blocking two hours for exercise seven days per week. That was a huge time commitment. To make it work I would multitask by using the two-hour run as strategy and thinking time. I went from enjoying a flexible diet and a glass of wine on most nights to a very disciplined diet with almost no processed foods.

After training for so long, the day of the marathon finally arrived. I ended up finishing slightly off of my goal at 2:37, which was still sub 6 minutes per mile for 26.2 miles. I started with a goal that seemed unimaginable, but it became a reality. Had I not picked the goal, told the world, hired a coach and run the miles, I'd still be a 3-hour marathoner.

Take these lessons and apply them to business. It's pretty simple: pick a goal that's unimaginable at the time; surround yourself with the right people and you will get better. Then, put together a plan and focus on the right things. Plan wisely by bringing only people around you who will rally behind you. Always give it everything that you've got. Once you're finished, be prepared to get better the next time! You just might find out that you were able to achieve more than you could have ever imagined.

Block Time For Your ONE Thing

Beyond having accountability points, leveraging habits to instill discipline is essential. Time blocks are one of the most basic habits that are incredibly powerful but terribly underutilized. Block time daily to spend on the most important activities. Discipline around prioritization further increases the effectiveness of those time blocks. One of my favorite disciplines around prioritization comes from a friend and mentor, Gary Keller, who recently authored a book titled The ONE Thing. The ONE Thing highlights that there is only ONE thing that matters most at any given point in time. It's a very simple, but powerful concept. Create the discipline to think about your priorities that way and do it daily. Make your goals real.

Visualize Your Vision

In an organization, visualizing your vision means posting the goals everywhere throughout the office. It means starting every internal (and external where appropriate) meeting by reinforcing those goals. It also means aligning every employee's compensation and goals to the BHAG of the business. This makes it real. When it is real, and when you focus, you will achieve what you set out to

accomplish. Changing the world is difficult, so do not do it alone. Take advantage of the infinite amount of resources and knowledge that is now available to us all thanks to a digital and highly connected world.

Never Give Up

Beyond believing and doing, the last piece of writing your own story is never giving up. You should never quit what you believe in. If you quit, you are finished. If you never quit, one of two things will happen: 1) you will succeed, or 2) you will learn and grow next time. Steve Jobs believed that he could create an amazing user experience by thinking differently. For decades, Steve and Apple met resistance and criticism (i.e., not supporting Flash, incompatibility with Microsoft products, closed environment), and even moments where they failed, but they never quit.

During those times, it becomes more important that you leverage your Stars (chapter nine) and your Community (chapter eight) for inspiration and focus. Whether you are inventing new software, building a real estate sales business, or going after a marathon personal record, the odds will be against you. There will always be naysayers. For every one person who believes in you, there will be ninety-nine others who do not. I remember the first time we landed a cover story with dotloop and the comments that the article generated. People who did not even know me were making assumptions about what kind of person I was, stating that our model was wrong, that big competitors would beat us to the punch, etc. You will accomplish what you put your mind to, regardless of what others may think.

Stay Committed

When you're writing your own story, know that you won't always accomplish everything and that things don't always work out as you plan, and that's okay. To that end, you also have to know where your commitments lie, ranked by priority, because not everything is deserving of the same treatment. For example, although my marathon goal was important, my career passions are more important to me personally. Going into training, I knew this and had to balance the outcome against that reality. If I was willing to give up everything else and commit 100% to running, I could have finished sub 2:30, but I wasn't ready for that. I was willing to commit 2 hours per day for 5 months and that commitment earned me a 2:37. Although 2:37 was less than my goal, I'm still proud of where I finished in context with my life's other priorities. Balancing commitment with reality and competing interests in life is an art, not a science.

At the end of the day, if you are committed to writing your own story and you are competitive, then something in you will always want to hit that goal. Ideally, you'll hit lots of them, but life is precious, and you live only once, so maximize the time by balancing what you are passionate about and what makes you feel the most fulfilled. Changing the world, building a real estate business or running a two-hour thirty-minute marathon is all tough work, but worth the trouble. So follow your passion and never give up. Peoplework companies write their own story, and never fail to go from one chapter to the next.

Reaching your goals and achieving your best potential may take longer than you would prefer. It's a never-ending journey. It may require more sacrifice than you are willing to make. But anything is possible if you want it bad enough; the challenge for most is that they do not want it enough to see the belief through that strenuous road to reality. Whatever you want to accomplish, you can.

The Rest Is Up To You

The stories of great entrepreneurs who were able to change, and innovate, the world around us are not stories of superheroes. Rather, they are examples of how everyday people looked beyond what was in front of them and what they were told was possible. They saw something deeper and they believed that they could change the world for the better. This is done only by understanding how people work, by understanding the community of people around you and how to make people's lives better. At its core, this is the essence of Peoplework.

The world is made of people like you and me; we can change it by writing our own story. Start by believing you can do it, visualizing it, and committing to doing what it takes to be successful and never give up.

Thanks to the Peoplework era, there really are no limits. The possibilities are endless! The Peoplework principles are the foundation of how you write your own story. In order for them to enable a limitless life, you must first believe and then go do it. Peoplework businesses write their own story and you can too.

PEOPLEWORK BUSINESSES WRITE THEIR OWN STORY AND YOU CAN TOO

Notes

i | http://blog.kw.com/2013/09/16/keller-williams-realty-becomes-largest-real-estate-franchise-in-north-america/

ii | http://en.wikipedia.org/wiki/Airbnb

iii | http://en.wikipedia.org/wiki/Taskrabbit

iv | http://en.wikipedia.org/wiki/Taskrabbit and http://en.wikipedia.org/wiki/Kickstarter

v | http://en.wikipedia.org/wiki/Toms_shoes

vi | http://en.wikipedia.org/wiki/Zappos

vii | http://www.businessweek.com/articles/2012-09-25/tesla-fires-up-solar-powered-charging-stations

viii | http://www.businessweek.com/articles/2013-08-29/why-amazon-is-on-a-warehouse-building-spree

ix | http://en.wikipedia.org/wiki/Ebay and http://www.forbes.com/sites/georgeanders/2013/05/22/meg-whitman-jolts-hp-as-its-reluctant-savior/

x | http://business.time.com/2013/04/09/the-5-big-mistakes-that-led-to-ron-johnsons-ouster-at-jc-penney/

xi | http://www.forbes.com/sites/alexknapp/2013/06/28/shotspotter-lets-police-pinpoint-exactly-where-a-gun-was-fired/

xii | http://en.wikipedia.org/wiki/Nest_thermostat and http://www.wired.com/geekmom/2012/12/nest-thermostat-review/

xiii | http://en.wikipedia.org/wiki/Houzz

xiv | The Starbucks Experience, by Joseph Michelli. McGraw-Hill, 2007.

xv | http://techcrunch.com/2010/05/28/video-evernote-ceo-phil-libin-shares-revenue-stats-and-how-to-make-freemium-work/

xvi | http://blog.kissmetrics.com/how-to-calculate-lifetime-value/

xvii | http://www.retailcustomerexperience.com/article/183007/Survey-Twice-as-many-people-tell-others-about-bad-service-than-good

xviii | http://www.businessinsider.com/chart-of-the-day-ad-spending-for-tech-companies-2010-5

xix | http://forbes.com/sites/languatica/2012/05/31/delivering-happiness-why-at-zappos-its-your-birthday-every-day/

xx | http://en.wikipedia.org/wiki/Southwest_Airlines

xxi | https://helpouts.google.com/111693949829020507693/ls/bb85af336deeda54

xxii | http://en.wikipedia.org/wiki/Square,_Inc.

xxiii | http://techcrunch.com/2012/03/17/the-real-sxsw-winner-is-the-mophie-juice-pack/

xxiv | http://venturebeat.com/2013/06/20/tripit-brings-its-headache-saving-team-travel-planning-to-iphone-and-ipad/

xxv | http://www.nytimes.com/2006/11/15/business/media/15adco.html

xxvi | http://www.sethgodin.com/sg/ and http://www.ted.com/talks/seth_godin_on_the_tribes_we_lead.html

xxvii | http://en.wikipedia.org/wiki/37_signals

xxviii | https://www.facebook.com/notes/the-facebook-effect-by-david-kirkpatrick/why-mark-zuckerberg-is-more-interested-in-growth-than-money-or-advertising/405208288253

xxix | https://www.dotloop.com/

xxx | http://curaytor.com/

xxxi | http://www.quickenloans.com/press-room/fast-facts/our-isms

xxxii | http://www.inc.com/allison-fass/peter-thiel-mark-zuckerberg-luck-day-facebook-turned-down-billion-dollars.html

xxxiii | http://www.fastcompany.com/1767793/creative-cultures-mailchimp-grants-employees-permission-be-creative xxxiv | http://money.cnn.com/2013/09/10/technology/steve-jobs-gift/ and http://www.youtube.com/watch?v=KuNQgln6TL0

xxxv | http://www.csa.com/discoveryguides/film/review2.php

xxxvi | http://www.hollywoodsgoldenage.com/hist.html

xxxvii | http://en.wikipedia.org/wiki/Over-the-Rhine

xxxviii | https://en.wikipedia.org/wiki/Doug_Collins_(basketball)

xxxix | http://en.wikipedia.org/wiki/Phil_Jackson and http://www.inc.com/magazine/19960901/1799.html

xl | http://en.wikipedia.org/wiki/Elon_Musk

xli | http://www.fastcompany.com/3022444/leadership-now/5-ways-to-reframe-your-thinking-to-be-more-like-elon-musk

xlii | http://www.apple.com/hotnews/thought-on-flash

AUSTIN ALLISON

Austin Allison is founder and CEO of dotloop, the fastest-growing technology company in real estate. After studying Real Estate Development at the University of Cincinnati and Corporate Law at The University of Cincinnati College of Law, Austin co-founded dotloop in 2009.

CHRIS SMITH

Chris Smith is the co-founder of Curaytor. Curaytor focuses on software, systems and support for salespeople. Chris co-hosts a popular weekly web show about marketing and technology called #WaterCooler. He was recently named the most influential person in the real estate industry. Chris serves as the Chief Peopleworker for dotloop.

We'd love to hear your thoughts on the book, you can contact us directly at:

austin@pplwork.com
@GAustinAllison

chris@pplwork.com
@Chris_Smth

PEOPLEWORK
RAISED
$73,280
on
KICKSTARTER

ALL THANKS TO
The Following People

Our Supporters

Samantha Spencer

Petra Quinn

Chris Nichols

linda hart

Sharona Byrnes

Heather H Holliday

Anna Child

Joe Pryor

Kim McNamara

TraceyThomas

Debi Raymond

Michael Thorne

Toni Reintke

Phil LeGree

Jim Marshall

Steve Overton

Patty Knaggs

Julie Chancerelle Ziemelis

Stephane Pujol

Mark JM

Giovanni Vajna de Pava

Ken Brand

Harry Moore

Jon Wade

Stefanie Ainge Hahn

Bill Madder

Will Hansen

Ron Zupko

Don Reedy

Lisa Daloise

Ryan Shields

Julie Misty Noland

Elad Rokach

Mary Winnett Giroux

Cliff Paulick

Jennifer Holden

Stephanie Lanier

Chad Humphrey

Daniel Gladziszewski

JKay Cha

Mike Incorvaia jr.

Kathy Riland

GeekAhead.Com

Josh Herst

Susan Mangigian

Scott Feirn

Susan

Patricia Harris

Tracy Weir

Christine Davis

Rhonda Carter

Heather Ozur

Samantha McLean

Caroline Carrara

Justin McHood

Steven Knapp

Tres Bradford

Laurie

Michael Gonzalez

Adam Gallegos

Jonathan Reese

Christine Hancock

Tristan Emond

Kevin Cunningham

Cat Humphries

Jacy Riedmann

Brandi

Aaron Huntley

Kathleen Sheridan

Anna Ryan

Kim Minor

Oscar S. Bowen

Hope Rosenberg

Sharon Alters

Loren Sanders

Joyce Van Den Berg

Sarah Toppins

Samantha

Steve Haas

Mindy Roiff Shanfeld

Christopher Russ

Lisa Kopp

Grant Goldfarb

Leif Eric Achée Fredheim

Tobias

Josh Schwartzberg

David Chiu

Zulliza Alizul

Michiko Romm

Nicolas Frot

Catherine Morgan

Nick Baldwin

Lee Adkins

Marjorie Tinnell

Sarah Herda

Katelyn Manning

Gwen Brindley

Marika Abuashvili

Andrea Geller

Terence Richardson

Edsel Burkholder

Missy Caulk

April Sullivan

Ron Farren

Suzanne Roy

Matthew Shadbolt

Katie Casey

Lindsay Bacigalupo Reuter

Gwen Daubenmeyer

Leslie B Jones

Cheri Paulsen

Suzette Colvin

Gregory Gerik

Michelle Poccia

Chris Ruszkiewicz

Lori Young Najera

Judy Atherton

Mary McKane

Virginia Dean

Cari Gennarelli

Chris Schilling

Dale Heuermann

Bill Faulkner

Eileen Colville

Charlie Carp

Vanessa E. Murray

Jennifer Goodman

Danai Mattison

leigh brown

Susan Ramirez Fleming

Marisa Mion Chisena

Molly chance

Treva Fox-Christy

Jason McCree Gentry

Wade Lester

Stacy Roby

Zach Pfeifer

Gene Krutyansky

Scott Forcino

Karen Taylor Williams

Steven Pahl

Kathie Gabriel

Arnold DeSena

Joe Schutt

Rich Bradford

Victor Lund

Kristina Moutz Cusick

John Popp

Katherine Karr-Garcia

Doug Francis

Rita Tayenaka

Bobbi Howe

Barb Joyce

Garrison Matte

Courtney Johnson

Kenneth Southworth

Linda Rosenthall

Bob Watson

Sandra Bundy

Patty Newell Mortara

Anne Jones

Jason Farris

Michele Wood

Gary Lingenfelter

Marilyn Urso	Cyndee Haydon
Matthew Dollinger	Jack Attridge
Isabel Garcia	Justin
Kevin Smits	Laura Doucette
Tony vehon	Joe Dahleen
David Bramblett	Leslie Jones
Ryan Bokros	Judy Klemm
Meghan McCarthy	Sam Powell
Marlow Harris	Robert Millaway
Martie Standish Abercrombie	Leslie Ebersole
Hugh Weber	Sue Adler
Sunny McCallum	Erik Kelly
Lisa Archer	Jeffrey Kershner
Debra Trappen	Susan Braaten
Tiffany Kjellander	Jeff Turner
Jeff Lobb	Kimberly Curtis
Mike Falls	Janie Sederberg
Grier Allen	Craig Schaid
Mark Passerby	Mike Bowler Sr
John Mangas	Jason Rose
Sean Moore	Nobu Hata
Chuck Smith	Mike Parker

Mary Krummenacher	Xplode
Bernadette Cole	Re/Max
Julie T. Farmer	Coldwell Banker
Gary Keller	Prudential Fox & Roach
Linda Davis	The Weiniger Group
Mark Burger	Greater Boston Association of
John Sweeney	Realtors
Jenni Davies	Placester
Linda Licause Hobkirk	Happy Grasshopper
Michael Wrabel	Kevin Tomlinson
Rosemary Buerger	YPN
Rich Bira	Listing-to-leads
Becky Jackson	Market Leader
David McCarthy	Follow Up Boss
Gloria Minnich	Middlesex County Association
Todd schroth	of Realtors
Evan Sage	
James E Martin	
Barbara Schmidt	
John Ziemba	
HousingWire	
Keller Williams	

ALONE WE CAN DO SO LITTLE;
TOGETHER WE CAN DO SO MUCH.

-HELEN KELLER

I'M NOT A BUSINESSMAN.
I'M A BUSINESS, MAN.

-JAY Z

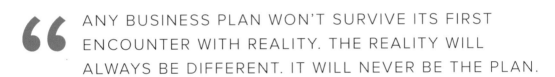

ANY BUSINESS PLAN WON'T SURVIVE ITS FIRST ENCOUNTER WITH REALITY. THE REALITY WILL ALWAYS BE DIFFERENT. IT WILL NEVER BE THE PLAN.

-JEFF BEZOS

EFFORTS AND COURAGE ARE NOT ENOUGH
WITHOUT PURPOSE AND DIRECTION.

-JOHN F. KENNEDY

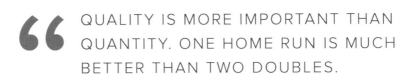

QUALITY IS MORE IMPORTANT THAN
QUANTITY. ONE HOME RUN IS MUCH
BETTER THAN TWO DOUBLES.

-STEVE JOBS

 NOTHING INFLUENCES PEOPLE MORE THAN A
RECOMMENDATION FROM A TRUSTED FRIEND.

-MARK ZUCKERBERG

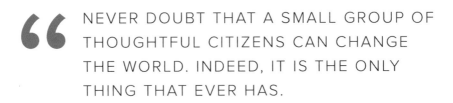

"NEVER DOUBT THAT A SMALL GROUP OF THOUGHTFUL CITIZENS CAN CHANGE THE WORLD. INDEED, IT IS THE ONLY THING THAT EVER HAS.

-MARGARET MEAD

INSTEAD OF WONDERING WHEN YOUR NEXT
VACATION IS, MAYBE YOU SHOULD SET UP A
LIFE YOU DON'T NEED TO ESCAPE FROM.

-SETH GODIN

THE STRENGTH OF THE TEAM IS EACH
INDIVIDUAL MEMBER. THE STRENGTH
OF EACH MEMBER IS THE TEAM.

-PHIL JACKSON

 THE DIFFERENCE IN WINNING AND LOSING
IS MOST OFTEN, NOT QUITTING.

-WALT DISNEY

PRINCIPLE 1
P2P REPLACES B2B AND B2C

PRINCIPLE 3
CHANGE NEEDS A BLUEPRINT

PRINCIPLE 5
QUALITY CREATES QUANTITY

PRINCIPLE 7
BUSINESSES ARE BUILT ON COMMUNITIES

PRINCIPLE 9
STARS ARE MADE IN HOLLYWOOD

PRINCIPLE 2
HUMAN COMPANIES WIN

PRINCIPLE 4
PURPOSE BEFORE TECHNOLOGY

PRINCIPLE 6
SERVICE IS MARKETING

PRINCIPLE 8
PASSION POWERS PROFITS

PRINCIPLE 10
ONLY YOU WRITE YOUR STORY

"An up-to-date new road map to success!"

Elena M Dagostino

"Outstanding and practical."

John Mangas (MetroToledoJohn)

"An easy, informative and great read."

Kirk R. Simmon

Easy read and very thought provoking.

T Walker

peoplework

Austin
Allison   ·   Chris
Smith